Reflections
of a
Domestic
Violence
Prosecutor

Reflections of a Domestic Violence Prosecutor
Suggestions for Reform
Michelle Kaminsky

© 2011, 2012 Michelle Kaminsky.
All rights reserved.

CONTENTS

INTRODUCTION	2	Addressing the Problems
PART 1	17	Misogyny and Stereotypes
	25	Battered Women and Stereotypes *People v. George Frazier*
	33	Women and Violence *People v. Turner*
	42	Misogyny *People v. Peter Fields*
PART 2	51	Mandatory Arrest and Prosecution
	56	No History of Violence *People v. Seth Clark*
	62	A History of Violence *People v. Paul Gordon*
PART 3	71	Obstacles to Holding Offenders Accountable: Working within the Adversarial System
	73	Legal Principles and Deterrence *People v. Charles Higgins*
	83	Judges and Defense Attorneys *People v. Thomas Cross*
	92	Mental Illness and Substance Abuse *People v. Henry Edwards*
PART 4	99	Safety
	101	Separation and Jealousy *People v. Hector Sanchez*
	107	Children and Financial Dependence *People v. Carlos Montero*
PART 5	114	A Successful Prosecution
	116	Achieving Justice *People v. Frank Brown*
	121	Conclusion
	124	Endnotes

In memory of my father, Carl I Kaminsky

Author's Note

The views expressed herein
are those of the author, and
are not necessarily the views of the
Kings County District Attorney's Office.
The names and identifying
characteristics of the people portrayed
in this book have been changed.

Acknowledgments

I would like to thank the following: Charles J. Hynes, the Kings County District Attorney, for taking a chance on me twenty years ago; Victor Barall for giving so freely of his time and editorial advice; Patrice McMahon, Sharon Wexler, Paul Beck, Raymond Beegle, Stacey Neumann, Sherry Fixelle, and Charles Murkofsky for their unfailing support and encouragement; Elizabeth Schneider for her knowledge and guidance; Danielle Atkins, Heather Florence, Sara Goodman, Bruce Green, Madeline Hoffer, Gloria Jacobs, Pure+Applied, Maggie Sandor, and Todd Shuster for their time and expertise; Wanda Lucibello, Judge Matthew D'Emic, Judge John Leventhal, all my colleagues and support staff, and the Victims Services Unit for their tireless efforts; Mark Hart for his love, support and belief in this project; and most of all Willa, for her delightful spirit, boundless energy and unconditional love.

INTRODUCTION

Addressing the Problems

I WAS NEVER much of a crusader. In the early eighties, when I was in college in Washington D.C., many of my fellow students protested daily in front of the South African Embassy, throwing themselves on the front lawn as a symbolic gesture against apartheid. Others lived in a shanty on the campus quad. In my junior year, the first intifada occurred. Arab students manned a television set in the student center with video taped footage of Palestinian children being shot with rubber bullets by Israeli soldiers. While I was outraged by these injustices, fear of arrest kept me from demonstrating. Instead, I would sympathize with the protestors over a cup of coffee in the student lounge.

At the time, I didn't realize that I could work within an established system to tackle injustice. The legal system, for me, had always been the world of my father, a copyright lawyer who made deals in glamorous places like the Cannes Film Festival. The law was his passion. I went to law school to connect with my father, not to address societal ills. In my mind, Cornell, my father's law school alma mater, was the portal to a worldly and sophisticated life, a life that I wanted. Unfortunately, Cornell saw otherwise and rejected my application. While Brooklyn Law School didn't hold the same prospects, it was the school that accepted me.

Brooklyn Law School is located right off of Court Street, close to the foot of the Brooklyn Bridge. Upper Court Street in the late eighties was a seedy strip. On one side of the street was the Blarney Stone, the local watering hole. By 11:00 a.m., the old timers were hunched over their respective bar stools, staring aimlessly ahead. On the other side of the street was a boarded up movie-theater and Pandora's Box, the adult video and book store.

It was the summer of 1989 when my brother and I drove over the Brooklyn Bridge for the very first time. Raised in the suburbs, we had never been, or thought about going, to Brooklyn. Now this outer borough was going to be my home for the next three years.

Hoping to catch some of the more scenic sights, we turned down Atlantic Avenue and drove for miles, right into the heart of Bedford Stuyvesant, a community known at the time for its gangs, drugs and murders. Just as we came to a red light a man wearing a long jacket crossed the street. He reached inside his coat right in front of our car, prompting my brother and me to dive for cover. We were convinced he was going for a gun, ready to blow us away. TV, an overactive imagination, and a sheltered existence brought out the worst in us.

Within a few short months, however, I grew to love the school, my professors and Brooklyn itself. I met Professor Elizabeth Schneider, an internationally recognized legal scholar on violence against women, in my second semester, when I took her course, Civil Procedure II. Towards the end of the term, she asked me to be her research assistant, a job I held until I graduated three years later.

Understanding violence against women to be the inevitable consequence of gender subordination, the battered women's movement of the early 1970s set out to transform the very laws and institutions that enabled men to batter. Professor Schneider was working on a report for the Ford Foundation on the status of these legal reforms.

Through my research I learned about the historical and legal developments that led to passage of mandatory arrest laws. Up until the mid 1990s, police departments across the country were notorious for their failure to arrest batterers, even if a woman was standing before them bruised and bleeding. As far as the police were concerned, it was a private matter to be resolved in the home. A confluence of events in the 1980s—including battered women[1] filing lawsuits against police departments for their failure to protect them—led legislatures and police departments across the country to change their policies.

Despite all the knowledge I acquired, I still never considered a career helping battered women, although I really didn't have anything else in mind, either. My career choice was actually a matter of chance. I was in the career placement office of Brooklyn Law School one day when I saw an advertisement for a position with the Kings County District Attorney's Office (also known as the Brooklyn District Attorney's Office), the agency responsible for prosecuting all violations of the New York State Penal Law within the confines of Brooklyn. The responsibilities of attorneys in the office ranged from criminal investigations to criminal trials. It sounded interesting, so I submitted a resume. My first interview took place at the law school and the next two occurred in the District Attorney's Office. Rumor had it that if you made it past those three interviews you were guaranteed a job when you met the District Attorney himself.

Meeting Mr. Hynes for the first time was intimidating. He was the chief law enforcement officer in Brooklyn and he sat in an enormous office on the 4th floor of the Municipal Building at 210 Joralemon Street. He looked like a politician, tall and distinguished with a conservative suit and short silvery hair parted to the side.

After examining my resume, he asked me what experience I had in the criminal law. "One class," I said.

"Are you taking the prosecutor's clinic?"

"What's that?" I asked.

His face showed his displeasure with my response. I later learned that the clinic worked in conjunction with the District Attorney's Office in assigning misdemeanor cases to law school students. They not only received course credit, but first-hand experience into the inner workings of the criminal justice system. I had nothing like that to show for myself. "Are you going to take my trial advocacy course next semester?" he asked.

"Yes," I said, enthusiastically shaking my head up and down. That concluded my interview.

Two months later I was sitting in Mr. Hynes' class. The goal of the course was to teach students how to deliver an effective opening statement and closing argument, two important functions of a trial.

On the first day, Mr. Hynes handed us the case file of a murder that occurred at the fictitious Truck Stop Cafe in Brooklyn. We were to use it for all our work. Every week a few students would have to get up before the class and deliver their assignment. My first one was an opening statement. With a touch for the dramatic I pounded on the top of the jury box in the moot courtroom to emphasize my point. Mr. Hynes looked pleased.

I finally got up the courage to approach him. "Uum, Mr. Hynes, I had an interview with you a couple of months ago but I never heard back from your office."

"I'll look into it," he said before walking out the door. The following week Mr. Hynes called me over. "Just keep doing what you're doing," he said with an encouraging smile. I breathed a sigh of relief.

It was May of 1992 when my home phone rang. "Is Michelle Kaminsky there?"

"This is she," I said.

"Please hold for the D.A." I couldn't believe it; the D.A. was calling me! I will never forget that day, when Mr. Hynes offered me a position as an Assistant District Attorney, starting in October of 1992.

By the time I started, I had been living in Brooklyn for three years. While I initially thought it was the epitome of urban squalor, I had come to love this county as much as the colorful Marty Markowitz who a few years later would become borough president and the inspiration behind such signage as "Welcome to Brooklyn, How Sweet it is," and "Leaving Brooklyn? Oy Vay!"

But my real feel for Brooklyn only came after I started working in the D.A.'s office. It was there that I became involved in the lives of many of its residents. One of the first units I worked in was the Investigations Bureau. The Bureau responded to all major crimes in Brooklyn, 24 hours a day, 7 days a week. Our mission was to enhance each case by interviewing witnesses and suspects immediately after the crime had occurred. Every fourth day a few of us would be on call. That meant that we had to spend the night in the office. There was one room that contained some beds. Rumors of bed bugs kept me from ever spending a night on one of them. Instead, I would bring a sleeping bag and park myself on the dirt-stained hallway couch, hoping not to swallow a chunk of the chipping paint that hung overhead. But it really didn't matter because we hardly slept. The calls would come in at all hours of the night.

It was a constant adrenaline rush—the thrill of being beeped at 3:00 a.m. to a homicide in East New York, arguably one of the roughest

There I was, a twenty-six year-old who had grown up in the safety of the suburbs, with my manicured nails and tailored suits, sitting in a cinderblock interrogation room with a killer who was now calmly answering my questions about the murder he had committed just a few hours before.

neighborhoods in the United States at the time. There I was, a twenty-six year-old who had grown up in the safety of the suburbs, with my manicured nails and tailored suits, sitting in a cinderblock interrogation room with a killer who was now calmly answering my questions about the murder he had committed just a few hours before. Nor will I forget the sixteen-year-old boy sitting in a holding cell of that very same precinct sucking his thumb as he waited to face charges for shooting up the street with his TEC-9.

Then there was the unforgettable ride down Knickerbocker Avenue as we headed to the 83rd precinct in Bushwick. "What's that?" I shrieked after hearing a succession of popping sounds. "Gun fire," the detectives calmly replied. Teenagers were firing off rounds on a nearby rooftop. "What are you doing?" they laughed as I took cover on the floor in the back of the car in my suit and heels. They thought it was funny; I thought I was going to die.

I was shocked by the nether-worldliness of those places: abandoned lots with burned cars and used tires strewn about, cashiers in the corner stores barricaded behind bullet-pocked Plexiglas, and young men on street corners selling drugs. Housing projects were everywhere: the Tilden Houses, the Pink Houses, the Van Dyck Houses, the Brownsville Houses, the Seth Lowe Houses, the Howard Houses, the Glen More Houses, the Cypress Houses. They were characterless brick buildings, tall and imposing. Then there were the churches that stood on every corner. I had never seen so many churches. Some were even inside store fronts, with signs proclaiming, "Jesus Saves." It was hard to believe that just a few short miles away lay the beauty of Brooklyn Heights.

Most of the cases from the Investigations Bureau took me to neighborhoods like these, where the poverty and crime were widespread. After leaving this unit I rotated through a few more bureaus before joining the Civil Rights Bureau. There I prosecuted bias−motivated crimes. The cases fell primarily into two categories: the racially motivated assaults and the racist and anti−Semitic graffiti writers. Back in the mid−nineties I was a regular at the 62nd precinct in Bensonhurst, a community rocked by several racial incidents.

One of my very first cases involved a young Italian street thug named Jimmy. Jimmy was in his early twenties when he stabbed two young Hispanic teenagers over some perceived slight as they walked out of a movie theater in Bensonhurst. "Niggers," Jimmy screamed, before plunging a knife into the chest of one, and the stomach of another. One day the police got a lead that Jimmy was inside his mother's apartment. I went with the detectives that night to observe them execute the arrest warrant. There I was, with my note pad and pony−tail, standing on a residential street with close to fifty armed uniformed officers wearing bulletproof vests. Members of the Emergency Services Unit ran up the stairs of the four−family brick home with machine guns and battering rams. I remember hearing the shouts, "PUT YOUR HANDS UP MOTHER FUCKER." I jumped behind the building and plastered myself to the brick, holding my note pad for protection.

In March of 1997, after two years in the Civil Rights Bureau, the Chief Assistant District Attorney called me to his office, informed me that the Domestic Violence Bureau was looking for more assistants and asked if I would be interested in a transfer. It's been fifteen years since I accepted the offer.

After joining the bureau, I participated in "New York Walks to End Domestic Violence," an event held during Domestic Violence Awareness Month in October. Hundreds of people walked through Riverside Park. Mariska Hargitay, a.k.a. Detective Olivia Benson of Law & Order's Special Victim's Squad, even came out to lend her support. There was a live band and all the participants received goodie bags from the various corporate sponsors. My favorite gift was the oversized long sleeve soft cotton t—shirt calling for an end to domestic violence. I wore that shirt until it was threadbare.

Over the years, I have noticed that same message calling for an end to domestic violence on advertisements in the subways and from public service announcements on television. I often wonder whether the public realizes just how difficult this message is to implement, especially within the confines of the criminal justice system.

I wonder if people know that the majority of women do not want to pursue criminal charges against their abusers, and that the majority of these cases end up dismissed or with non—criminal dispositions. I wonder if people know that abused women are not helpless victims, as the battered woman's syndrome paradigm suggests. I wonder if people realize that criminal prosecution is an imperfect solution and will never be the means to eradicate violence against women. And I wonder whether people are aware of the larger social and economic context in which most of the domestic violence that I handle occurs, a context which includes inadequate housing, wages, health care, and education, substance abuse and mental illness, isolation due to non—immigrant status and insufficient resources and support services to address these needs.

When I first started in the Office in 1992, the Domestic Violence Bureau was housed in a small corner on the second floor of the run-down Criminal Court building. Mice and dust bunnies shared with us the limited floor space. Most of the misdemeanor domestic violence cases were handled before one judge. He fancied himself a comedian and used a microphone in court. "Be nice to the lady," or "Use the golf club on the green not on her head," he would say. It was disturbing to watch the offenders laugh as the judge minimized their criminal behavior and, at the very same time, the experiences of the women who had been battered.

Back then, domestic violence was also treated with disdain among assistant district attorneys in my office. There was this belief that anyone who was sent to the Domestic Violence Bureau was being punished. Except for the few people committed to the cause, no one ever volunteered to prosecute those cases.

ADDRESSING THE PROBLEMS

I wonder if people know that the majority of women do not want to pursue criminal charges against their abusers, and that the majority of these cases end up dismissed or with non-criminal dispositions.

Over the past twenty years, there has been a shift in attitudes toward domestic violence, both within my office and from the public at large. Due to the efforts of the battered women's movement, there have been tremendous legislative and judicial reforms on the national, state and local levels. Battering is now seen as a serious crime and treated accordingly. In fact, criminal prosecution has become the primary means of dealing with this crisis. A strong law enforcement response is premised on the belief that the criminal justice system can hold batterers accountable and keep women safe. Many states, including New York, have mandatory arrest laws for batterers, and pro–prosecution policies for domestic violence crimes.

Brooklyn has been in the forefront of this change, with the first felony domestic violence court in the nation opening there in 1996. Now the borough has three such courts. Under the leadership of District Attorney Charles Hynes, the Brooklyn District Attorney's Office started a Domestic Violence Bureau in 1990 with a full time staff of social workers. In 2005, the Office received a grant from the United States Justice Department to house a Family Justice Center.[2] The Center provides a wide range of civil services for battered women, including legal services for divorce, custody, child support and immigration matters.

Despite these reforms, the criminal justice system doesn't seem to be reducing domestic violence or providing meaningful change to its victims. I believe the reasons for this are threefold. First, the very nature of the criminal justice system undermines its ability to bring about meaningful change. Second, the goals of the criminal justice system are often in

> *The criminal justice system is an adversarial system. It's a system that views everything in black and white, with little room for compromise. It's prosecutor versus defense attorney, victim versus offender, guilty versus innocent.*

direct conflict with the wants and needs of battered women. And finally, there is a lack of resources to effectuate meaningful change.

The criminal justice system is an adversarial system. It's a system that views everything in black and white, with little room for compromise. It's prosecutor versus defense attorney, victim versus offender, guilty versus innocent. It's a system where statistics are paramount; statistics regarding how many trials the judge presided over and how many convictions the prosecutor obtained. It's a system where defense attorneys often confuse and manipulate facts in the name of zealous advocacy, and where "expert" witnesses obscure the truth. It's a system that requires the prosecutor to bear the burden of proving the defendant's guilt, despite the very real injuries inflicted on the victim. And it's a system that can't rehabilitate violent misogynists, or guarantee a woman's safety.

The criminal justice response to domestic violence is premised on the assumption that all battered women want to leave their batterers. This is a faulty assumption. While women want the battering to end, they do not necessarily want their abusers prosecuted, or for that matter, their relationships to end. Most women just want their batterers to get "help."

Battered women are far more concerned with safe, affordable housing, living wages, and child care, than they are with criminal prosecution. In fact, many women fear that prosecution will interfere with these basic needs, since arrest and prosecution of a batterer can lead to financial hardship, loss of child care, and in some cases, further violence.

ADDRESSING THE PROBLEMS

While the Family Justice Center is supposed to address these primary needs, the resources to do so are scarce. The vast majority of women that end up in the Domestic Violence Bureau are young, poor, uneducated, single, minority women with small children. Living wages and safe housing are virtually non–existent for them. I have been to many of their homes. I have witnessed the broken locks that enable prostitutes and drug dealers to do business in the hallways. I have ridden in the urine soaked elevators, and walked through the dark maze–like hallways. But I have always done so with two armed detectives.

Despite the reforms of the past twenty years, there are still judges on the bench who are either ignorant of the dynamics of abuse, abuse their own power, or engage in overt sexism. In some ways, this behavior is more insidious than the actual violence because it feeds the culture that sanctions violence against women. The real irony is that judges often engage in these behaviors in front of the very offenders who are in court for their own abusive behavior towards women.

To further complicate matters, judges, just like juries, have a tendency to view these cases, and make decisions, based on stereotypes about women in general, and battered women in particular. The most common are that battered women are weak, helpless and psychologically disturbed, and that women in general are incapable of unprovoked acts of violence.

These stereotypes are fed by sensational cases like Hedda Nussbaum, the Random House editor who was brutally beaten by her boyfriend in the 1980s, and made–for–TV movies like the "Burning Bed," in which Farrah Fawcett played a woman, who after suffering years of abuse at the hands of her alcoholic husband, set him on fire. Such cases become etched in the public's mind and end up defining what an abused woman looks, sounds and behaves like.[3]

The cases that I handle, however, bear scant resemblance to the ones that make the tabloids or end up on the big screen. Over 90% of the approximately eight thousand domestic violence cases handled in Brooklyn each year involve "low level" criminal offenses, like threatening telephone calls, name calling, hair pulling, shoving, punching, slapping, and spitting.

I too have been guilty of stereotyping. My biases, like most people's, are a product of my environment, the way I was raised. While I grew up in a socially progressive household, my mother had her beliefs. Like the way she believed that the Jews could do no wrong. If a person happened to be an alcoholic, gambler or general no-goodnick, and Jewish, my mother would mention the Jewish part in a whisper, the way some people do when discussing cancer.

Maybe that's why I was so riveted by the story of a woman I met at a fundraiser at the Harvard Club. She told me how her first husband beat her. I had heard hundreds of stories of abuse over the years, yet I couldn't get over hers. The same thought kept running through my head, "A wealthy Jewish businessman from Park Avenue beats his wife."

In the process of writing this book, I came to see how my own biases affect my thinking. Like how I believed I was different from the women I was helping. The truth, however, was that I had been in my share of troubled relationships. While mine weren't violent, I would still get this gnawing sensation in the pit of my stomach whenever I heard about the fights—the cursing, the put downs, their partner's drinking. I knew about those fights. I lived them. Ironically, I always asked the women why they just didn't leave, when I myself continued to stay. As if I didn't know about the fear of being alone, of the belief that something is better than nothing.

I finally left one particularly painful relationship because I had the money to get my own place, the support of loving friends and professionals and no children to bind me. Most of the women I work with are not as fortunate.

The reality was that I was confronting some of the very same issues in my professional life that I had dealt with in my personal life. It was hard to acknowledge that connection, between their stories and mine. After all, I was the prosecutor, they were the victims. For so long, my perspective towards my cases was driven by the belief that I knew better.

That belief started to unravel as I began to look outside of my own limited understanding of battering. I started to read works by battered women's scholars and advocates. That's when I started to see how my thinking, and approach to my cases, was problematic. I began to see how the seemingly innocent questions that I am constantly fielding—such as "Why does she stay?" or "Why doesn't she cooperate in the criminal prosecution?"—shift the blame for the abuse onto the woman. In my fifteen years prosecuting these cases, I don't think anyone has asked me

ADDRESSING THE PROBLEMS

...seemingly innocent questions that I am constantly fielding—such as "Why does she stay?" or "Why doesn't she cooperate in the criminal prosecution?"—shift the blame for the abuse onto the woman. In my fifteen years prosecuting these cases, I don't think anyone has asked me "Why does he batter?" a question that would place the blame directly where it belongs, on the batterer.

"Why does he batter?" a question that would place the blame directly where it belongs, on the batterer.

    I realized how I too have engaged in victim blaming by my incredible frustration when I would encounter any opposition from the victim to the prosecution. I was so caught up in doing my job, in prosecuting the batterer, that I failed to ask myself what it really means to help women who have been battered. I also failed to appreciate the complexity of their situations, of having to choose between prosecuting their lover/batterer or steering clear of the system so as to avoid that choice. And I failed to appreciate their resilience, to acknowledge the incredible strength it takes to survive amidst so many formidable obstacles.

    I have also come to see how mandatory prosecution policies feed the belief, at least within the criminal justice system, that battered women are psychologically disturbed. Such policies often pit prosecutors against the very women we are trying to help. Rather than question the soundness of a policy that so many battered women oppose, or acknowledge the economic and social context in which battered women make their choices not to proceed, the knee jerk reaction is to blame them for not going along with a policy that has been deemed to be in their best interest.

I have heard prosecutors in other jurisdictions justify mandatory prosecution as a means to "cover their asses." This was the rationale of one southern prosecutor I met at a national domestic violence conference. She boasted to the attendees how she had a battered woman arrested and jailed when she refused to cooperate. Her reasoning: "I was just covering my ass."

I don't fault this prosecutor. In fact, I appreciated her candor. She had the courage to acknowledge the untenable position of a domestic violence prosecutor. Prosecutors are public officials who are held publicly accountable. If a woman is injured because we failed to follow through on a case, regardless of a victim's wishes, we will be held responsible. I would be a liar if I didn't acknowledge how this truth affects my decision making process. How I have proceeded with cases despite the wishes of women because of that reality.

The truth is that battered women have little say when they come in contact with the criminal justice system. At the district attorney's office, women are told about the criminal process. If they don't want to participate, they are either told that the case will go forward without them, or that the charges will eventually be dismissed. They are then asked if they want to speak with a social worker about their "other issues," the very issues that often drive their decision not to pursue criminal charges.

I too have been guilty of approaching my cases like an assembly line worker, ushering women out of my office to meet with a social worker on any issue that did not involve the criminal prosecution, so that I could address the "real" issues, the legal ones. I simply failed to see how fundamental those "other" issues were.

The irony is that despite all the reforms of the past thirty years, battered women are often disempowered by the very system that is supposed to help them, while their batterers are often empowered by the very system that is supposed to hold them accountable.

ADDRESSING THE PROBLEMS

The irony is that despite all the reforms of the past thirty years, battered women are often disempowered by the very system that is supposed to help them, while their batterers are often empowered by the very system that is supposed to hold them accountable.

On the pages that follow, I use eleven cases to illustrate how societal beliefs about women, inadequate laws, judicial biases, inflexible prosecution policies and a lack of resources prevent meaningful change for battered women in the criminal justice system. While these are formidable obstacles, reform is possible if educators, prosecutors, judges, legislatures and the media work to bring about change.

To begin, prosecutors need to start incorporating battered women into the decision making process by listening to their wants and needs. While prosecution may be appropriate in some cases, it may not be the best approach in all cases. Prosecutors should also develop collaborative interdisciplinary response teams to address the complex social, economic and psychological issues present in many domestic violence cases.

On the judicial front, the selection of domestic violence judges must be made by judicial screening committees composed of various participants in the criminal justice system, as well as domestic violence organizations, rather than leaving selection to the sole discretion of administrative judges. This is the only way to ensure that the most qualified judges are handling these complex cases.

The judiciary must also hold batterers accountable when they engage in abusive, coercive and intimidating behavior during the pendency of a criminal case. Judges have the power to strip batterers of their constitutional right of confrontation if they engage in such behavior, and judges should use that power when the facts so warrant. Legislatures need to understand that domestic violence crimes, unlike stranger crimes, are unique because of the ongoing nature of abuse. Jurors need to hear about the history of abuse in order to have a proper context for understanding the specific crime for which the batterer is charged. This means that state legislatures must pass laws allowing for the admission of prior abuse at trial.

Since safety for battered women is fluid, risk assessments need to be conducted at various stages in the process to get a more accurate picture of the level of danger a woman faces. The level of danger posed by an offender must be a criterion in setting bail. Moreover, funding for the equipment and monitoring of global positioning systems (GPS) is an essential part of safety planning, enabling the most dangerous offenders to be watched twenty-four hours a day, seven days a week.

Addressing misogynistic beliefs and behaviors is a critical part of reform efforts. Educators and the media can play a crucial role in challenging socially constructed attitudes about gender. Children need to be educated about gender equality from the moment they enter school until they graduate, with a continuing curriculum running from kindergarten until twelfth grade.

Popular culture by way of television, movies and music continues to perpetuate regressive stereotypes about women and inaccurate stereotypes about battered women. This content creates a climate conducive to violence against women. The media needs to critically assess the content they are disseminating and actively work to raise public awareness to these issues.

Finally, Family Justice Centers have provided essential services to battered women, improving their lives for the better. In order to ensure the viability of these centers, the federal government and respective states must ensure a steady stream of funding.

1

Misogyny & Stereotypes

THROUGHOUT HISTORY, efforts to address domestic violence were limited by society's unwillingness to intervene in the family. The family, with its strict hierarchical roles of male breadwinner and female homemaker, was seen as a sacred institution to be preserved at all costs. In her history of family violence policy, Elizabeth Pleck identifies three points in U.S. history where domestic violence was publicly addressed: Colonial times, the Temperance Movement of the nineteenth century, and the Battered Women's Movement of the 1970s.[4]

In seventeenth century Colonial America, domestic violence was considered a threat to the stability of the family and the community.[5] Under the common law doctrine of marital unity, a wife's legal identity "merged" with her husband's upon marriage, giving him rights to her person, property, and labor.[6] While violence was condemned, a husband had the right to use "legitimate" physical force to punish a wife.[7] The law thus drew a distinction between women deserving of community protection, and unruly women deserving of physical punishment.[8] When cases of abuse were brought to the attention of Puritan courts, victims were encouraged to reconcile with their abusers in order to maintain the family.[9] Divorce for physical cruelty was a rarity.[10]

During the temperance movement of the 1840's, reformers targeted alcohol as the cause of domestic violence.[11] Banning liquor was seen as a way to protect women and preserve the family. Feminist reformers, like Elizabeth Cady Stanton and Susan B. Anthony, went a step further, demanding legislation authorizing divorce for battered women, custody of their children and the right to their own earnings.[12] They framed the issue in terms of a woman's right to be free from male violence, rather than the evils of alcohol and the sanctity of the family. Since their efforts were perceived as an attack on the family and male supremacy, they ultimately failed.[13]

By the end of the nineteenth century, the doctrine of marital unity began to erode as women gained the right to their own property and to sue on their own behalf.[14] The law no longer recognized a husband's right to use physical punishment against a wife.[15] Still, while judicial opinions condemned violence by husbands, the legal system refused to intervene on the grounds of marital privacy.[16] In one oft–cited judicial opinion, the North Carolina Supreme Court held, "If no permanent injury has been inflicted, nor malice, cruelty nor dangerous violence shown by the husband, it is better to draw the curtain, shut out the public gaze, and leave the parties to forget and forgive."[17]

Battered women had few options. The legal system not only effectively immunized their batterers, but denied them a means of escape by refusing them the right to divorce.[18] Battered women who managed to leave their husbands still had to figure out ways to adequately support themselves and their children. Yet, jobs for women at the end of the nineteenth century were extremely limited, and social support services were scarce.[19]

Between the temperance movement and the battered women's movement of the 1970s, domestic violence was not publicly addressed. Instead, psychiatry, under the influence of Sigmund Freud, took up the matter in the early twentieth century. Women's psyches, not men's violence, were targeted, and women's claims of early childhood sexual abuse, came to be understood as nothing more than fantasies, born out of their secret desires to have sex with their fathers.[20] Helene Deutsch, a disciple of Freud's, added to the misogyny by attributing female victimization to women's masochistic tendencies.[21] By first denying the reality of rape and incest, and then blaming women for the violence inflicted upon them, modern psychiatry legitimized the belief that women lie and provoke male violence.

Born out of the political movements of the 1960's, the battered women's movement of the 1970s not only challenged the prevailing psycho–analytic theories, but challenged the "family ideal,"[22] claiming that for many women the family was a dangerous place.[23]

Del Martin, in her 1976 book, *Battered Wives*, brought to light the horror women were experiencing behind closed doors. While police statistics from major urban cities highlighted the sheer scale of the crisis, domestic violence was not publicly addressed.[24] Martin documented law enforcement's indifference to the plight of battered women and the lack of social services to aid them.

In *Battered Women and Feminist Lawmaking*, Elizabeth Schneider describes the political nature of the Battered Women's Movement:

> First, "battered women" were set forth as a definable group or category, with battering regarded within the larger context of "power and control"; physical abuse was a particular "moment" in a larger continuum of "doing power," which might include emotional abuse, sexual abuse and rape, and other maneuvers to control, isolate, threaten, intimidate, or stalk. Battering, and the problem of power and control, were understood within a systemic framework as part of the larger dilemma of gender subordination, which included gender role socialization; social and economic discrimination in education, workplace, and home;and lack of access to child care. Battered women and battered women's experiences were the focal point of strategies for change; battered women were viewed as "sisters", actors, participants in a larger struggle. Their needs for safety, protection, refuge and social and economic resources drove the movement.[25]

Yet, many in the movement understood that in order to get the necessary political support to fund shelters and other social and legal services, reform had to be presented in a manner that did not appear too controversial. Since feminism was considered a radical ideology attacking the traditional family order, an alliance between conservative feminists and politicians was formed, resulting in domestic violence being treated as a law and order issue.[26]

> *Domestic violence, however, is a complex social issue that defies easy quick fix solutions from the criminal justice system.*

Domestic violence, however, is a complex social issue that defies easy quick fix solutions from the criminal justice system. Academics from varying disciplines can't even reach a consensus as to its causes and cures.[27] Sociologists, for example, believe that violence between intimate partners is the result of structural conditions like poverty and unemployment, which place enormous stress on families,[28] whereas psychologists see violence in the home rooted in individual psycho–pathology.[29] Feminist scholars on the other hand, believe that violence against women is rooted in gender subordination.[30]

The extent and nature of domestic violence is also subject to dispute as is the gender of its offenders. Figures regarding the prevalence of domestic violence derive from population and point of service surveys, which vary depending on the questions asked.[31] For example, some surveys have shown that women are just as violent as men.[32] But these findings have been subject to extensive criticism, with commentators arguing that the methodology of the surveys and the questions asked fail to capture the context, consequences and meaning of the violence.[33]

The criminal justice system is also limited in its reach. It can only punish behavior, not beliefs like misogyny, which is the belief system that drives battering. For batterers, women are liars, whores, provocateurs, and bitches who deserve to be beaten.

Popular culture perpetuates misogynistic beliefs with corporate media reaping exorbitant profits by exploiting sexist stereotypes, and promoting the objectification of young girls and women.[34] Violence against women is excused by Hollywood and glamorized by pornography and sexually violent video games.[35] Then there is the music industry, profiting off of its "bitches" and "ho's" lyrics, and sexist videos of beautiful young women gyrating around an all powerful male.[36] These ever present images create an atmosphere conducive to violence against women.

Stereotypes about battered women, developed in psychology and reinforced by popular culture, pose additional problems.[37] Despite the reforms of the past thirty years, the same historic beliefs of deserving versus undeserving victims exist in our culture and are held by judges and juries who decide these cases. Battered women who are perceived as weak and timid are deserving of protection; battered women who are perceived as outspoken and assertive are believed to have gotten what they deserved.[38]

Then there is the backlash from men's rights groups who claim that female victimization is overly exaggerated to the detriment of male victims.[39] While I have no doubt that men underreport domestic violence due to shame and stigma, I question whether men experience abuse in the same way as women given that violence against women has been tolerated throughout history and endorsed by popular culture.

While mandatory arrest laws and pro-prosecution policies have lifted the historic veil of family privacy, little has been done to address the very attitudes that drive the behavior.[40] As Del Martin presciently observed 35 years ago, domestic violence "will never be solved until a radical change is effected in prevailing attitudes about women..."[41]

Education is critical for shaping beliefs for future generations, and a powerful means to counter the troubling messages that children receive either at home, in popular culture or both regarding women's subordinate status. At least seven states have laws urging or requiring school boards to develop curriculum on teen dating violence.[42] Legislation for such curricula is pending in other states.[43] In my opinion, however, it's far too late, and too limited in scope. Teen dating violence is already a serious social issue, with one out of four adolescents reporting verbal, physical, emotional or sexual abuse from a dating partner each year.[44] Gender role socialization and the message of women's subordinate status takes place early in a child's development.[45] This means that we need to reach children at an even earlier age, and for their entire education with a continuing curriculum, running from kindergarten through twelfth grade, that addresses gender equality as well as healthy relationships.[46] The Center Against Domestic Violence, a New York City based organization, has taken on this mission by creating age appropriate programs for elementary, middle school and high school students.[47]

> *ScenariosUSA is another high school program doing ground-breaking work...*
> *...their curriculum addresses issues such as socially constructed gender norms, intimate violence, sex, and sexuality. By fostering meaningful classroom discussion, the students think, reflect upon, and question their belief systems.*

"Relationships are Elementary," targeting fourth and fifth graders, is their thought-provoking curriculum developed in partnership with the Bank Street College of Education. The program is currently operating in one school in Brooklyn. "Speak Your Peace," which operates in four middle schools, focuses on healthy relationships that are free from bullying and abuse. RAPP—"Relationship Abuse Prevention Program"—operates in twelve high schools in New York City and has reached thousands of teenagers. In addition to an educational program on abusive relationships, counseling services are provided by a social worker and teenagers are trained to be peer leaders under the belief that teenagers are more likely to listen to other teenagers when it comes to relationships.

ScenariosUSA is another high school program doing ground-breaking work.[48] Operating in three regions of the United States—New York City, Cleveland, Ohio, and the Rio Grande Valley of Texas—their curriculum addresses issues such as socially constructed gender norms, intimate violence, sex, and sexuality.[49] By fostering meaningful classroom discussion, the students think, reflect upon, and question their belief systems. The students are encouraged to write their thoughts in journals, and turn their journal writings into a project for publication.

Every two years, ScenariosUSA sponsors a writing competition, pairing the winning students with Hollywood directors who turn their work into short films. The films are extremely thought provoking, featuring teenagers dealing in a mature way with the very same complex social issues addressed in the classroom.

Challenging beliefs and attitudes also requires educating the public about the realities of domestic violence and its victims. There have been numerous national and international public awareness campaigns over the years, with one earning a Silver Lion Award at the Cannes Lion International Advertising Festival.[50] Yet, public awareness campaigns by their very nature are superficial. They are not designed to expose the complexities of social issues.[51] We need to impart substantive information to the public so that society has an accurate understanding of the scope and content of the crisis. The media can play a critical role by using its power and reach to portray real victims, not stereotypes.[52] Every medium, from television, broadcast journalism, movies, radio, music, newspapers, books, magazines, blogs, and social media sites, should be used in order to reach a large swath of the population.[53]

Domestic violence could be tackled on soap operas, which have been used in other countries to address numerous social issues.[54] Through thought provoking lyrics, music can address the complexities of domestic violence, using its influence to reach millions of listeners nationally and internationally.[55] England is using the airwaves to address domestic violence, with the BBC broadcasting a radio drama called "Believe Me", in which issues of control, jealousy, trust and violence are explored in an abusive relationship.[56]

Reality television is a leading genre that has begun to tackle social issues like teen pregnancy, in MTV's "Teen Mom", to drug addiction, in A & E's "Intervention". If a non-exploitative program were developed that profiled real women in abusive relationships and the multitude of issues they face from education, to jobs, to finances, to child care, to the effects on their children, society would gain a more realistic understanding of their plight.[57] The program could also focus on efforts to address the crisis by interviewing domestic violence organizations, religious leaders, feminist scholars, policy makers, criminal justice officials, sociologists, psychologists and politicians. This way the sheer breadth of the issue and the varying responses to it could be conveyed to the viewing audience.

The more media that get involved in addressing this epidemic, the greater our chances of creating a paradigm shift in attitudes and beliefs towards women in general and battered women in particular.

Battered Women & Stereotypes
People v. George Frazier

GEORGE FRAZIER WAS facing life imprisonment. If I could convince a jury of his guilt, he would be off the streets, no longer a threat to women.

George Frazier and Betty Lopez grew up in Bedford Stuyvesant Brooklyn, a neighborhood ravaged by drugs in the 1980s. Betty was addicted to crack cocaine and sold it to support her habit. In the early 1990s, she was convicted of felony sale of a controlled substance and sentenced to two and a half years' imprisonment. She left behind five young children. Betty got a break when the state diverted her to a treatment and work program. After a year and a half, she came home clean.

Betty was independent, driven and assertive; the polar opposite of the image of the battered woman: weak, timid and helpless.[58] She managed to turn her life around and earn a certificate from a local technical school as a home health aide. Betty also devoted herself to raising her children, and eventually, her grandchildren.

George met up with Betty a few months after he was released from prison. A few weeks after they started dating, George moved into her apartment. There was tension in the house from the moment he arrived. Betty's children didn't like him and after one particular argument, Betty's seventeen–year–old daughter, punched him in the face. Betty asked George to leave after that incident, but he refused.

Almost immediately, George began accusing Betty of cheating on him. He would show up at her workplace and call her throughout the day.

He was constantly pressuring her to have sex. Most of the time, Betty would acquiesce just to keep George quiet. Sometimes, however, George would lock Betty in the bedroom and force her. He would pull her hair and hold her down, knowing she would never scream because she didn't want to frighten her children.

Betty eventually would come to learn about George's criminal history. Back in the late 1980s, George had sliced a girlfriend in the face when she tried to break up with him. When she wouldn't get back together, he threw a Molotov cocktail into her kitchen window. For that act, George would serve three years in prison, followed by another two years for a parole violation. One year after his parole expired, he set another girlfriend's apartment on fire when she tried to break up with him. For that act, he served seven years. Four months after his release, he met up with Betty. Seven months after his release, he set her apartment on fire.

Betty spent Christmas of 2005 at her oldest daughter's home. George came along. George's mother kept calling him on his cell phone. "Leave me alone bitch," he yelled each time. George became extremely agitated and told Betty that he was going back to the apartment. Betty went with him because she was afraid that George would run into her teenage daughter, and given their history, she didn't want him alone with her.

As soon as they got inside, George started hitting and pushing Betty towards the bedroom. He told her to take off her clothes. When she wouldn't, he ripped them off and then climbed on top of her and raped her. He repeatedly punched her in the head while he was inside of her. When he was finished, he went to her dresser, picked up a bottle of rubbing alcohol and threw some on her vagina and the rest on the mattress. He then went to the hallway closet and retrieved a container of lighter fluid. That's when Betty threw on her pants and shirt and ran down a flight of stairs to her neighbor's apartment.

George ran after her with a knife in one hand. "Get back here bitch," he screamed. As Betty banged on her neighbor's door, George grabbed her by the pony tail, pulling her towards him. Just as Betty was struggling to break away, her neighbor, Stephanie, opened the door and kicked George in the groin. Betty ran inside Stephanie's apartment and slammed the door. As Stephanie spoke with the 911 operator, you could hear George banging on the door, and Betty screaming "you stupid asshole."

Betty came outside when she heard the police in the hallway. They wanted to know why there was blood in the vestibule area by the front door. Apparently, George got cut in the hand during the struggle. Betty was upset and talking fast. The police interpreted what she said as if she had confessed to stabbing George. As they asked her to step outside, they all heard what sounded like a gun shot. That's when they all ran out. Minutes later, smoke was pouring out of Betty's front windows followed by flames.

Betty tried to run inside but the police held her back. The firefighters were able to save her two cats but nothing else. Every baby picture, every graduation photo, every school diploma, every stitch of clothing and furniture that belonged to Betty and her children was destroyed that night. She had no insurance.

Betty had been raped and assaulted, and watched her home go up in flames. She didn't think it could get worse until the police arrested her for stabbing George. But George wasn't even there since he managed to escape right after he set her place on fire.

Back at the precinct, Betty explained to the police that George had started the fire but didn't tell them about the rape. As a result, Betty never went to a hospital for a sexual assault examination. She would later explain to a jury the reason why she remained silent; she was ashamed and embarrassed.

A few hours later, George walked into the precinct with a bandage on his hand. He told the police that he had a fight with Betty and that she had set her mattress on fire. The police then arrested George, leaving it for the District Attorney's Office to sort out.

Betty spent three nights in jail. After I consented to her release, Betty came to my office with her attorney and told me what had happened. The 911 call, her neighbor, Stephanie, and George's criminal history, all supported what she said. Based on all that information, I went to court and dismissed the charges against her.

George was a serial arsonist. He had two prior felony convictions for arson. This was his third violent felony offense. If convicted, he faced a maximum term of life imprisonment.[59] This time George refused to plead guilty, figuring he had nothing to lose by taking his case to trial.

I found myself questioning my obligations as a prosecutor. How far was I supposed to go to build my case against George? Was I supposed to lose my humanity in the process?

Since George was claiming that Betty started the fire, the Judge ruled that the jury had the right to know about George's history of setting his prior girlfriend's homes on fire. After that favorable ruling, I went looking for George's victims. With a little digging, detectives from my office located Dionne. Fifteen years had passed since George sliced her face with a knife and tried to set her home on fire with a Molotov cocktail.

I sat with Dionne for an hour talking about the upcoming trial and her relationship with George. The scar on her face was still visible. Towards the end of our conversation, she told me about the night he cut her face. "I looked into his eyes that night and I saw evil. I can't see him again. I'm sorry, but I just can't," she said.

I had the power, through a material witness order, to have her arrested and brought before the court.[60] I found myself questioning my obligations as a prosecutor. How far was I supposed to go to build my case against George? Was I supposed to lose my humanity in the process? Was traumatizing Dionne merely a collateral consequence of doing my job effectively? I saw first hand how George had physically and emotionally scarred her. In the end, I couldn't bring myself to do it, so I left her alone.

I then started my search for Susan, the girlfriend from George's second arson. She had moved out of state but with a few computer searches, and the aid of her local police department, I got her telephone number. Susan wasn't surprised by my call. She said she knew he would do it again. I asked if she would come to New York to testify at the trial. At first she was willing, then she was scared, then she got angry. She began reliving her own experiences, how she was alone with her kids in a shelter with no support after George burned down her home.

I had two detectives fly out to speak with her because Susan kept going back and forth during our many telephone conversations. In the wee hours of the morning, after talking for many hours, Susan agreed to come to New York.

Betty took the witness stand and told the jury everything that George had done to her that night. Betty wasn't a victim in the traditional sense of the word; she was a survivor who was assertive and direct.[61] Betty had a tendency to use street slang. When I questioned her about the rape and asked her where George had put his penis, she responded by calling her vagina her "punany nany." On another occasion, when describing the pain she felt after George threw rubbing alcohol at her, she pointed between her legs and stated that her "thang thang" was burning. Some of the jurors were laughing, others sat there stoically. Betty's mannerisms and mode of speaking were simply inconsistent with the stereotype of a battered woman.[62]

The defense attorney went after Betty on cross-examination, discrediting her as a drug-addicted felon who would do anything to get what she wanted. When Betty explained that shame and embarrassment kept her from telling the male police officers about the rape, the attorney confronted her about all her prior encounters with the police when she was using drugs, and asked whether she felt embarrassed then. Ultimately, he argued to the jury that women like Betty don't feel shame. Women like Betty are manipulative, dishonest and cunning. They simply can't be trusted.

Susan testified, followed by Stephanie, Betty's neighbor.

George was the last person to take the stand. He wore a conservative button-down shirt and a pair of khaki slacks. It was hard to convince a jury that he was a rapist, batterer and arsonist when he looked like he walked out of a Brooks Brothers catalogue. He was calm and soft spoken in contrast to Betty, whose speech was rapid and slang-filled. George claimed that because Betty knew about his prior arson with Susan, Betty had set her own apartment on fire and then framed George so she could get him out of her life.

The irony is that we ask our citizens, through the jury system, to judge the facts of a case free from bias and prejudice, when inevitably juries filter the facts through stereotypes. Jurors, like most people, have an uncanny ability to flip off the switch, refusing to see the complexity of their own lives or the "messiness of [their] own intimate relationships" when they sit in judgment of others.

How the jury could believe such a claim, that Betty would destroy everything she owned just so she could frame a man she had been dating for a mere three months, was incomprehensible. Yet, the jury bought it, and acquitted George of all charges.

After the trial some court room observers told me that Betty wasn't "likeable." Another told me that she was "too sassy."

If Betty didn't appear like a sympathetic victim when she testified, the jury should have seen her when she learned about the verdict. "No it can't be," she cried. "He's going to kill me and my kids."

I had detectives pick up Betty and her children and bring them to my office. I'll never forget how frightened Betty was that night. She sat in a chair across from my desk rocking back and forth as tears streamed down her face. "He's going to kill me," she kept saying. For a time she was inconsolable.

My office was prepared to do everything necessary to keep her safe, including housing her and her children in a hotel until we could relocate them. After a few hours, however, Betty returned to herself. With her children by her side, she told me that she wasn't going to let that "mother fucker" destroy her life; she was staying at her job and going back home.

I couldn't make Betty into something that she wasn't. I couldn't mold her into the paradigmatic victim.[63] But that didn't change the fact that George had raped her and set her home on fire. She told her story in her own voice. It was the jury who chose to discredit her because she didn't live up to the stereotype.[64]

The irony is that we ask our citizens, through the jury system, to judge the facts of a case free from bias and prejudice, when inevitably juries filter the facts through stereotypes.[65] Jurors, like most people, have an uncanny ability to flip off the switch, refusing to see the complexity of their own lives or the "messiness of [their] own intimate relationships" when they sit in judgment of others.[66]

Given this reality, how can we do better to ensure that victims like Betty receive justice, and men like George are held accountable? The answer is to confront the stereotype of the "battered woman" head on in both law and culture.

Education and the media are critical for confronting and challenging cultural beliefs, while jury selection is the way to do it in the courtroom. Prosecutors need to address with jurors what their beliefs are regarding victims of domestic violence; what they envision a person who has been victimized to look like, speak like, and behave like. We need to ask juries why stereotypes exist and acknowledge how stereotypes fail to capture the complexity of human beings. We also need to confront the way "victim" is shrouded in historic notions of pure chaste women deserving of protection and belief, versus sullied women who lie and get what they deserve.[67]

We need to confront the agency/victimization dichotomy, which holds that a person is either an agent of their own destiny, operating with free will and choice, or a victim being acted upon.[68] This dichotomy fails to acknowledge the complexity of human beings and their relationships, and that people can be victims and agents at the very same time.[69] This false dichotomy results in juries holding women like Betty responsible for their own victimization under the belief that they should have made better choices. Yet, one's ability to exercise free choice depends upon one's

...ular circumstances. Choice does not operate in a vacuum. Betty's ...noices were limited by the fact that she was trapped in a violent relationship and lacked the means and the resources to get away from George.[70]

We need to educate our culture and juries that women like Betty can be tough talking and independent and still be victims, deserving of help.[71] If we fail to confront this fact in our society, and by extension with our juries, we will continue to lose cases because jurors will continue to disbelieve women who fail to live up to the stereotype.

Women & Violence
People v. Diane Turner

DIANE WAS SITTING next to her lawyer wearing a mint green suit with her oversized bible prominently displayed on the table in front of her. She was trying to convey to the jury that she was a woman of God, righteous and devout as she stood trial for murdering her son's father.

Gregg Winston was an engineer. He was handsome and muscular and 6'4" tall. Friends and family all described him as a sweet gentle man. One friend even nicknamed him the Gentle Giant.

Gregg was twenty-four when he met Diane. She was six years older. Monogamy was not his strong suit. His indiscretions would end up costing him his life.

The extent of his infidelity was on full display in the courtroom as one woman after the other took the witness stand, describing her relationship with Gregg and her encounters with Diane. First was Leslie, Gregg's high school sweetheart. He was still seeing her when he started dating Diane. Diane put an end to that by bombarding Leslie with telephone calls letting her know that Gregg was now her "man." The phone calls stopped the day Leslie broke up with Gregg.

Then there was Sonia, a woman Gregg met on a bus. She was beautiful, tall and thin, with long, curly hair. She looked like she had walked out of a fashion magazine. She, too, was the victim of Diane's harassing phone calls. "You want to die over a black nigga? Keep seeing my man because you will die," Diane said to her on the phone one night.

REFLECTIONS OF A DOMESTIC VIOLENCE PROSECUTOR

A few months later, Diane was pregnant. Gregg, however, continued to see Sonia, keeping Diane's pregnancy a secret. When Sonia finally learned about the baby, she ended her relationship with Gregg.

Gregg's mother and father sat in the courtroom throughout the trial, listening to the details of Gregg's relationships, hearing the defense portray him as a scheming philanderer. At the end of each day of trial testimony, Gregg's father would stand with me in the hallway of the courthouse going through the day's events, emphasizing everything that was positive. His mom was so soft spoken. She would just stand there leaning on her cane as her husband waved his hands while making his points. There was this look of resignation on her face, knowing that her only son was never coming back.

Back in 1999, Mrs. Winston had called the police when Diane refused to let Gregg leave his apartment. In 2002, as I was getting my case ready for trial, I spoke with the police officer who responded. He had responded to hundreds of 911 calls since that day but he still remembered the look on Gregg's face when he went to their door. He just couldn't get over the fact that someone of Gregg's stature could be that afraid of a woman.

About 10% of the eight thousand domestic violence cases handled in Brooklyn each year involve female defendants. Sometimes I really feel for them, especially when they have children. Like Francine Holmes, a woman I prosecuted years ago for killing the father of her kids. Francine was a heavy drinker with an explosive temper. She was drunk the night she confronted John in front of her house, accusing him of cheating. She got right up in his face. That's when John punched her in the mouth, behavior that was out of character. Francine ran inside her house, grabbed a knife and then ran back into the street and plunged the knife into John's chest.

The crime scene photos showed the knife block in the kitchen right next to the refrigerator which was decorated with colorful magnetic letters of the alphabet; the same letters my sister-in-law keeps on her refrigerator for my niece and nephew.

It would have been easy to dismiss this woman as a ruthless killer. But she wasn't. I remember her arrest photo. There she was standing by the cement wall of the precinct with urine stains running down her light denim jeans. She was so frightened that she had wet her pants.

WOMEN & VIOLENCE

About 10% of the eight thousand domestic violence cases handled in Brooklyn each year involve female defendants. Sometimes I really feel for them, especially when they have children. Like Francine Holmes, a woman I prosecuted years ago for killing the father of her kids.

Francine sometimes brought her young children to court, the little boy in a stroller, the little girls in Mary Janes and colorful bubble gum looking beads hanging from their braids. They were adorable.

"What will happen to them if their mom goes to jail," I often thought. I tried to wipe those thoughts away, constantly reminding myself that Francine had killed a man. It wasn't always easy to do.

A jury convicted her of the least serious charge, Manslaughter in the Second Degree, and she was sentenced to a year and a half in jail. Francine's temper cost her children their father. She would have to live with that for the rest of her life.

I was never able to empathize with Diane, however. She was cold and manipulative, and I never got the sense that she felt for anyone but herself.

The stories of Diane's explosions were endless. Like the time she showed up at the Winstons at 2:00 a.m banging on the door demanding that Gregg come home with her. Then there were the constant phone calls to Leila, the new woman in his life. "You whore, you'll never have him," Diane would scream.

By the early summer of 2001, Gregg was making plans to marry Leila. They went to the Caribbean and when they returned they went apartment hunting. Gregg, however, was still sleeping with Diane, and by July she was pregnant again.

Gregg's behavior, like the behaviors of so many people in intimate relationships, was inexplicable. I once had a male victim who sustained second degree burns to over 25% of his body after his ex–wife poured battery acid on him. He lost an eye and needed a skin graft. After spending six weeks in the Cornell Burn Unit, he started having "phone sex" with her even though she had been indicted for felony assault. When I asked him why he would speak with her after she disfigured him so severely, he simply shrugged his shoulders as if to say "I don't know."

At the end of August 2001, Gregg went to the Family Court and applied for an order of protection after Diane threatened to kill him and Leila if he ever left her. On Friday August 30, 2001, three days before his murder, Gregg packed all his clothes and left a note on the kitchen table telling Diane that because she made it so difficult for him to leave in person, he was letting her know by letter that he couldn't take her behavior anymore and was leaving for good.

After finding the note, Diane walked out of the apartment and went to stay with her girlfriend in Queens. She left her teenage daughter, who was visiting from South Carolina, and her autistic child to fend for themselves.

On Monday morning, September 3, 2001, Diane called Gregg's parents crying, claiming that she missed their son and that she needed to see him. The Winstons told her that they would contact Gregg. When Diane called back, she was told that Gregg would go to her home at 3:00 p.m.

Gregg planned on serving Diane with the order of protection that day. Family Court orders of protection, unlike Criminal Court orders, require the recipient to have the opposing party served with the initial court order.[72] That morning Gregg went with his sister to the local precinct, hoping that a patrol officer would serve it. But it was the West Indian Day Parade, leaving the precinct with no available officers. Gregg's sister Karen would serve the order.

At around 3:00 p.m., Gregg and Karen pulled up in front of the house. Diane was waiting for them out front, dressed in a tight fitting skirt and top, holding a Coach pocketbook. Karen sat in the back of the Ford Expedition while Diane sat in the front passenger seat. "Consider yourself served," Karen said as she handed Diane the Family Court papers.

Diane refused to acknowledge them, letting them fall to the ground. "Why do you always have to make everything so difficult?" Karen demanded.

That's when Gregg asked his sister to step out of the car so he could speak with Diane. Karen sat down on the stoop a few feet away and made some calls on her cell phone, arranging to meet up with her friends.

Five minutes later, Karen heard two shots ring out and then saw Diane jump out of the car and run down the block. Gregg was sitting in the driver's seat motionless, with his safety belt fastened, his head falling forward, blood spilling from the side. The cigarette was still hanging from his mouth. He was shot once in the chest and once in the head. A 22-caliber revolver was lying on the front passenger seat.

By the time the police arrived, Diane was gone. The detectives arranged to fly down to Diane's family's hometown in South Carolina on September 11, 2001. Due to the events of that day, they never made it. It would be another month before they could look for her. Five days after the detectives came back they received a phone call from Diane's lawyer. She was back in New York, ready to turn herself in.

Detective John Hayes of the Brooklyn South Homicide Squad was assigned to this case. For most detectives their work would have ended the day they made the arrest. Not Detective Hayes. He continued to uncover information in order to help me build my case. Because of him, I learned that Diane had been arrested years earlier in the Thirtieth Street Train Station in Philadelphia for possession of a loaded semi-automatic pistol. I also learned that Diane was fired from a previous job with an insurance company for stealing money from a co-worker's bank account. She fought with the head of human resources, demanding to know why they wouldn't pay her for her unused vacation time.

"So I get nothing," Diane said.

"No, employees terminated for cause are not eligible for a vacation cash out," said the director.

"Well, what's terminated for cause? I don't even know what that is."

"Employees terminated for cause have violated a company policy," said the director.

"What policy did I violate? Look I don't have my handbook with me. What policy? I didn't break a company policy. I stole from Nicole. I didn't steal from the company. So, I didn't break a company policy then, did I?" she indignantly replied.

The more Detective Hayes uncovered, the more I learned about her character; how she was devoid of a conscience.

I remember seeing Detective Hayes months later in a police precinct, waiting for his colleagues to finish up their paperwork. A bunch of the precinct detectives were cracking jokes near the Osama Bin Laden poster that read "Wanted Dead or Alive." Detective Hayes was quietly sitting in the back of the precinct reading the *New York Times*. He was an exceptional detective.

Diane was without emotion the day I interviewed her in the precinct. She wanted me to believe that the gun belonged to Gregg and that he tried to kill her in the car. According to her story, the gun accidentally went off when she managed to grab the gun before Gregg could reach for it. There was just one problem with Diane's story: Gregg was shot execution style, with the gun directly to his head. How does that happen by accident?

Diane was held without bail and sent to Rose M. Singer, the women's jail on Rikers Island. That's where she gave birth to her daughter. The baby stayed with her until she was one and then went to live with Diane's mother in South Carolina. Sometimes I think about that little girl and wonder what she will tell her friends when they ask an innocent question like "Where were you born?" Will she tell them that she was born in the largest penal colony in the world?

About a year later, the judge offered Diane a plea to Murder in the Second Degree with a sentence of twenty years to life, five years less than the maximum. Gregg's family was in court, hoping for some closure the day she admitted to her crime. But Diane would once again deprive them of the very thing they wanted most. A few days later, Diane's lawyer managed to get the plea withdrawn. He argued that Diane had been pressured by her family because they couldn't afford his fees. The judge allowed her to take back her plea and set the case over for trial.

The trial testimony was damning, with scientific evidence proving that the second gunshot was fired intentionally, rather than accidentally, as Diane had claimed.

Then there was Diane's re-enactment of the crime. As she sat on a chair in front of the jury box, dramatically re-enacting the struggle, she proved to the jury that the crime could not have happened the way she claimed, that it was physically impossible for her to bend down and retrieve the gun from under the seat if Gregg was choking her.

Judge O'Brien refused to charge the jury on self-defense as the defense attorney requested, finding no credible evidence to support it.

Within two hours, the jury returned a verdict of Murder in the Second Degree. The next day the Daily News had a quote from the jury foreperson regarding Diane's claim of accident: "If one wound could have been accidental, the second took all error out of it."

Even after she was convicted, Diane tried to manipulate her way out of a life sentence by writing a letter to the judge in which she commented on his "smile of encouragement", and said that she hoped he would show "mercy and leniency" so she could go home and mother her infant daughter. The judge saw right through her, sentencing her to twenty-five years to life.

Postscript

Two years later, in March of 2005, the New York State Appellate Division reversed Diane's conviction, finding that Judge O'Brien committed error when he failed to charge the jury on the law of self-defense. According to the Court, there was a "reasonable view" of the evidence that Diane had in fact acted in self-defense.

A few years prior, the very same Court, in another case of domestic violence, found that a trial court did not err when it refused to give a self defense charge for a man accused of killing his girlfriend.[73] From my reading of the two court opinions, the only real difference was the gender of the accused.

On November 3, 2005, four years after Gregg's murder, Diane was re-tried. She had been sitting in Bedford Hills Correctional Facility for close to two years, no doubt studying those transcripts from the first trial, rehearsing how she would testify the next time around. This time she was much more polished. The drama from the previous trial had vanished. She now claimed that when she shot Gregg she was trying to defend her life. She never used the word accident. By the second day of deliberations the jury was deadlocked. Two jurors were swayed by her claims; ten were not. The judge had no choice but to declare a mistrial.

While gender role socialization dictates that women are passive nurturers, family violence researchers have found women to be just as violent as men. Feminist scholars, however, have critiqued their methodology, claiming that the research fails to capture the context in which women use violence, and fails to show how men's use of violence has far more devastating consequences for women ...

    That meant a third trial for Diane. It also meant that the Winstons would have to relive the horror of their son's murder yet again. Unwilling to do that, they agreed to a plea deal: Manslaughter in the First Degree with a sentence of fifteen years.

    The tortured history of this case is not surprising given the conflicting data about women's use of violence. While gender role socialization dictates that women are passive nurturers,[74] family violence researchers have found women to be just as violent as men.[75] Feminist scholars, however, have critiqued their methodology, claiming that the research fails to capture the context in which women use violence, and fails to show how men's use of violence has far more devastating consequences for women than women's use of violence has for men.[76]

    Moreover, the findings of the family violence researchers are inconsistent with crime, safety, and point of service surveys like police departments, shelters, and hospital emergency room visits, which find men to be the dominant offenders.[77]

To add to the confusion, family violence research findings have been used by men's organizations to further their own political agendas.[78] This has led to public confusion of the issues, claims that women over-exaggerate the extent of violence against women, and a reduction of services for battered women.[79]

Sociologist and battered women's expert, Evan Stark, in his book *Coercive Control: How Men Entrap Women in Personal Life*,[80] explains the reason for these inconsistent findings: the researchers are tapping into different phenomena. Stark explains how family violence researchers are capturing, "common couple violence" where men and women use violence to respond to specific situations rather than as a means to control and subjugate their partners.[81]

Crime, safety and point of service surveys, on the other hand, are identifying what Stark refers to as "coercive control" which is "a range of tactics to control, isolate, and intimidate as well as injure partners," and which is used almost exclusively by men to dominate women.[82]

Stark's findings are consistent with what I have seen as a prosecutor. In Brooklyn, women far outnumber men as victims of intimate abuse, with over 90% of the cases in my Bureau involving male offenders. Moreover, male offenders tend to use verbal, sexual, psychological and physical abuse as a means to control their partners.[83] Female offenders, on the other hand, typically use violence out of anger to respond to a specific situation, not as a means to subjugate their partners.

While there are certainly costs to engaging in discussions about female violence—like men's rights groups using it to advance their own agendas—failure to do so merely perpetuates false notions about womanhood, which ultimately hurts battered women. This means that we need to challenge stereotypes about women and violence the same way we need to challenge stereotypes about battered women. The media, in all its forms, needs to raise public awareness to the matter in a socially responsible way.[84] Prosecutors, in turn, must address this issue in the courtroom by challenging historic notions of female passivity, one jury, and often one judge, at a time.

Misogyny
People v. Peter Fields

On July 24, 2002, John Taylor was driving a rental car in Brooklyn when the police pulled him over for failing to use his turn signal. Inside the glove compartment was a 40 caliber semi-automatic pistol with fifteen rounds in the clip. John was arrested and brought to the local precinct. That night he told the police that he knew the whereabouts of a woman missing from Flatbush since May. In exchange for a deal, he would lead them to her.

It was close to 2:00 a.m. when detectives headed out to a charred, shingled, abandoned house in East New York that was surrounded by a chain link fence and overgrown weeds. Burnt plywood hung in the windows. The roof consisted of a jagged spray-painted cement structure. It was the perfect refuge for the neighborhood crack addicts.

The floorboards were so weak that the detectives had to wait for a specialized unit of the police department to retrieve the construction size black garbage bag that lay on the trash-strewn floor next to a broken chair back and coffee table. Inside were the decomposing remains of a human body.

Early the next day, the medical examiner identified Tina Johnson by the tattoos that were still visible on her leg. Her six year-old son's name was written inside the heart shaped design.

John Taylor's statements would lead the police to Tina's boyfriend, Peter Fields, and his two cohorts, Steven Greene, an alleged member of

> *Fields' lifestyle resembled the set of a rap music video, with expensive cars, designer clothes, flashy jewels and beautiful young women. I couldn't tell who was emulating whom. Was Fields living out the fantasy of the videos, or were the videos glorifying the world Fields inhabited?*

the Crips, and Kevin Dexter, a lifetime parolee. By late in the day on July 25th, all three would be facing murder charges in her shooting death.

Tina met Peter Fields when she was seventeen. He was thirty-four. She was standing at the bus stop when he pulled up in his Cadillac Escalade. A year later, she was pregnant with his son. Fields was already married, with a daughter just a few years younger than Tina.

I immediately noticed the Prada and Burberry shopping bags in the crime scene photos of Fields' bedroom. His criminal ventures, most notably identity theft, supported those expensive tastes.

Fields' lifestyle resembled the set of a rap music video, with expensive cars, designer clothes, flashy jewels and beautiful young women. I couldn't tell who was emulating whom. Was Fields living out the fantasy of the videos, or were the videos glorifying the world Fields inhabited?

All of Fields' cohorts disrespected women. One in particular evinced a deep hatred of them.

"What can you tell me about Fields' relationship with Tina?" I asked.

"Tina was his wifey," he said.

"What's a wifey?"

"She's below a legal wife but above a girl you sleep with," he said.

"Was Fields faithful to her?"

"No," he said in disbelief at my question.

"We picked up girls in strip clubs," he added.

He then told me how they would sleep with the same women.

"Pussy's pussy. You can get it anywhere so why not share among friends," he said matter−of−factly.

Tina's sister gave me her photo. There she was in the middle of summer in a pair of shorts, standing by a car with a huge smile, hugging her little boy. Tina wanted to give him the best education so she sent him to a private school. Yet, Tina was merely a sales clerk in a music store owned by Fields. She was dependent on Fields for almost everything, including a roof over her head and her son's tuition.

Steven Greene and Kevin Dexter would put the pieces together. They would explain to a jury how a beautiful young woman's body was left to rot inside eight construction size garbage bags.

Kevin Dexter was thirty−seven and a three−time felony offender on lifetime parole. He was in custody at Rikers Island when I had him brought to my office. This career criminal who spent close to ten years of his life in prison whimpered and pleaded every time I met with him. "Pleeeeeeeeeeeeease let me out of jail." "I promise I'll come back." "I have to see my wife." "Are you married?" "She'll leave me if I can't see her." Three quarters of every meeting were spent listening to him moaning for his freedom.

Kevin met Fields at the DMV in Brooklyn. That's where Fields was working. Fields had a prior conviction for credit card fraud yet he was working at a government agency with unlimited access to personal information on the residents of New York State. Apparently no one at the DMV bothered to do a background check.

Only twenty−four, Steven Greene was not yet a hardened criminal like Kevin. Although he worked as a maintenance worker for a big corporation, in his spare time he hung out with "Crips, a Blood dude, and a Latin King." But Steven insisted that he was not a member of any gang, claiming that he wasn't strong enough to go through the grueling initiation process, which included a beating by every member of the gang.

These were the only people who would testify and say what happened the night Tina Johnson was shot five times in the head and chest.

Greene provided the motive for the murder as he explained the extent of Fields' jealousy. Fields was convinced every man who came into the music store was sleeping with Tina so he taped Tina's phone conversations, watched her on a television monitor, and incessantly accused her of cheating.

At around midnight on May 2, 2002, Steven got a call from Fields. When Steven went over to the house, he saw Tina lying on the floor, the top half of her body covered in construction size garbage bags. "Yo, it's over. I had to do it. She was living foul. I had to murk her. She was disrespecting me," Fields said. Steven was like a translator. I was always asking him to explain what he had just said. Foul meant cheating. Murk meant murder.

Tina's little boy was in his bedroom behind a closed door. I never knew what he saw that night because days after the murder Fields sent him down south to live with family. He was still there at the time his father went on trial for murdering his mother.

Steven claimed he was too frightened to help clean up, telling Fields to call Kevin, which he did. They then drove to Kevin's and brought him back to the apartment. Steven sat in the living room watching the two of them pull up the carpeting and padding and place them inside some garbage bags. They then carried the bags, including the one with Tina's body, down the steps and put them in the trunk of Fields' Escalade.

It was close to 2:00 a.m. when the three of them drove around Brooklyn looking to dump the evidence. On the way, Fields stopped at his daughter's apartment, walking out of the car with the gun in his waistband. When he returned the gun was gone. They continued to drive, stopping at a dumpster behind a housing project, where they unloaded the bag with the carpeting. They then headed out to East New York to the abandoned house. Kevin and Fields carried Tina's body out of the car and pushed the bag through the front door of the house. She was left there to rot during the hottest days of summer.

Three months later the police found her body. By that time, Fields had gotten rid of everything that could connect him to the murder. On the night he was arrested, the Crime Scene Unit, armed with a search warrant, went to Fields' home and ripped apart the floors and the walls looking for traces of blood and gunshot residue. The only thing they found was a coat of fresh paint and newly laid carpeting.

Rumors swirled in the neighborhood about sounds of gunfire that night. But no one would come forward. They were all afraid of Fields. Kevin and Steven would be the sole witnesses at the trial. The only two who could connect Fields to Tina's murder. In exchange they received pleas to Hindering Prosecution for helping get rid of Tina's body. Steven was sentenced to probation; Kevin was sentenced to one to three years in prison.

As a witness, Kevin was a prosecutor's worst nightmare. He was prepped for trial four times. He could have been prepped twenty times; it wouldn't have mattered. His voice was barely audible. Everyone in the courtroom was straining to hear him. "Keep your voice up," the judge kept saying. That afternoon I brought a microphone to court. I felt doomed, watching the microphone shake in Kevin's trembling hand.

Unlike Kevin, Steven was articulate and well composed on the witness stand. But there was no way of getting around his shady lifestyle. His associates were violent gang members. And months before the homicide, he had been arrested for possessing a gun. Unfortunately, I didn't get to choose my witnesses.

The following day Fields' younger brother, Gary, testified. He had spent seven years in prison for possessing a gun and selling drugs.

When I asked him if his brother thought Tina was disrespectful, he broke out into a misogynist rap, letting the jury know how he just ignores "his woman" when she argues because he's "the man."

Gary claimed that Fields was with him at the time of the murder. According to Gary's story, on the evening of May 1, 2002, he went with Fields to a lawyer's office to watch Fields refinance his building. Gary was there as an observer, wanting to see how things worked, since he was thinking about "getting into real estate." After the papers were signed, Gary, Fields, the lawyer and the mortgage broker celebrated at a local restaurant. At about 11:00 p.m. Fields picked up Tina and their son from her sister's apartment and dropped them off at home. Gary and Fields then returned to the restaurant. That, Gary claimed, was the last time they saw Tina.

On the following day, the real estate lawyer testified in court, confirming that Fields had been in her office that night with his brother. There was just one glitch that they didn't anticipate. The lawyer would reveal that an individual claiming to be Ed Connors, the brother of Peter Fields, signed the mortgage papers.

The judge and I looked at each other with furrowed brows. "Who's Ed Connors?" Ed Connors was none other than Gary Fields. He not only lied during his trial testimony, but he committed fraud in the real estate transaction, using a fake New York State driver's license. The license no doubt procured through Fields, who worked at the DMV.

"If you don't get him back here by tomorrow I'm striking his testimony," the judge warned Fields' lawyer. Fields was sitting in his expensive designer suit, wearing his hair in short tight braids. For the first time he looked scared.

The next day Gary walked into court. The bravado of the prior day was gone. With a court appointed attorney by his side, Gary asserted his fifth amendment right against self-incrimination to every question I asked him about his part in the mortgage fraud.

The defendant's main witness was an exposed liar. But that didn't matter. After a day of deliberations, the jury acquitted Fields of murder.

"Mr. Fields, you just got away with murder," the judge said before releasing him from custody.

I went to the jury room to find out why they let him off. I felt sick listening to them. "Well, we all thought that he did it, but didn't think you proved it beyond a reasonable doubt," they said.

"What else did you need?" I asked.

"The gun," one of them said.

"But he had three months to get rid of it," I said.

"Well, how do we know someone else didn't do it," they replied.

"Who else had the motive to kill her?" I asked in disbelief.

There was no response, just a collective blank stare.

This case wasn't just about a brutal murderer getting away with his crime, and the risks he posed to every woman he would encounter. It was about what Fields and his cohorts represented. Their misogynistic beliefs are the very reason men perpetrate violence against women.

Tragically, these beliefs are not just held by some small criminal element in our society. They are part of the fabric of our society and exist on a continuum. I have even encountered them in various degrees from the very members of the judiciary who decide these cases.

Moreover, domestic violence is not just a phenomenon occurring in poor inner city communities. Domestic violence affects all socio—economic classes.[85] Access to resources merely enables people of means to stay out of the criminal justice system.

Let us remember the following facts when we are quick to dismiss violence against women, and the beliefs that fuel it, as merely a social ill affecting poor communities and communities of color: that corporate media conglomerates, composed of powerful white males, reap billions of dollars a year promoting and exploiting sexist stereotypes that are embraced by popular culture;[86] that the majority of consumers of hip hop music, a multi billion dollar a year industry, which often denigrates women, are non—black;[87] that young men of privilege on private school and college campuses throughout the United States are committing violent acts against women;[88] and that even venerable institutions like Yale University have abusers in their midst.[89]

Corporate media has tremendous power to change the discourse about women. Yet, profit drives them to do otherwise. Jennifer Pozner, in her book, *Reality Bites Back, The Troubling Truth About Guilty Pleasure TV*, documents how reality producers take a premise that is "steeped in some social belief" and then exploit it, like the subordinate status of women.[90]

> According to Pozner,
> *reality television has emerged as American's most vivid example of pop culture backlash against women's rights and social progress...reality TV producers, casting directors and story editors have collaborated to paint American women as romantically desperate, matrimonially obsessed and hypertraditionalist in their views about the proper roles for wives and mothers, husbands and fathers.*[91]

In order to ensure that message is received loud and clear by the television viewing public, producers provoke fights, engage in highly selective casting, spend hours editing and cutting footage, and "Frankenbite", a process where statements are cut and pasted together.[92] National news then turns around and presents that manufactured message as fact.[93] For example, NBC's *Today Show* recently did a piece

Corporate media needs to be held accountable. Politicians who staunchly support the Violence Against Women Act need to publicly address the way corporate media contributes to the subordinate status of women. Why not start a dialogue with the big six media owners, at Viacom, News Corp, Disney, Time Warner, General Electric and CBS...

on women in reality television.[94] Rather than bring in an expert like Pozner to explain how these shows exploit stereotypes for financial gain, NBC interviewed a Los Angeles based psychotherapist, and a *TV Guide* employee. What the viewing audience was told by these two "experts" is that women, by their very nature, are competitive and jealous. Whereas men, have the ability to admire and support one another without feeling threatened.

NBC did a great disservice to women by running that piece the way they did. After all, if women are catty, mean, insecure and emotionally unbalanced, why should they be entitled to the same opportunities as men? And if women are so unglued, what's wrong with giving them a slap or two?

Corporate media needs to be held accountable. Politicians who staunchly support the Violence Against Women Act need to publicly address the way corporate media contributes to the subordinate status of women. Why not start a dialogue with the big six media owners, at Viacom, News Corp, Disney, Time Warner, General Electric and CBS, regarding the way reality shows from *The Bachelor* to *Who Wants to Marry a Millionaire*, perpetuate the worst stereotypes of women and thus foster a climate that results in violence against women. Maybe then we will see a shift in the way the media portrays women.

2

Mandatory Arrest & Prosecution

THE BATTERED WOMEN'S MOVEMENT of the 1970s challenged the conventional wisdom that domestic violence was a private matter.[95] Started by activists and survivors, the movement provided a feminist analysis of battering in which abuse was the result of male hegemony in the public and private sphere.[96] A core principle of the movement was a woman's right to self–determination and physical integrity. As such, reform efforts were guided by the specific needs of battered women as articulated by battered women. In addition to helping abused women obtain access to essential services like shelter, the movement was committed to changing the political and social conditions that led to women's subordinate status.

State agencies, like police departments and prosecutors' offices, were seen as complicit in the abuse, as both institutions had official policies treating domestic violence as a private family matter.[97] The police either failed to respond to women's calls for help, or when they did, responded inadequately.[98] The battered women's movement set out to make violence against women a matter of public import, and to ensure that state agencies treated domestic violence the same as stranger violence.

Yet, early activists understood the limits of criminal justice reform and the risks involved in engaging with the state. As Susan Schechter noted in her history of the movement, the criminal justice system "cannot end the conditions that create or perpetuate violence...[or provide] battered women with the economic and social resources—jobs, child care, housing,

Criminal prosecution was not seen as a solution to battered women's problems but as a "necessary aid[s]".

and safe communities—that they need to free themselves from dependence on violent men."[99]

Criminal prosecution was not seen as a solution to battered women's problems but as a "necessary aid[s]".[100] With that understanding, state coalitions, composed of various domestic violence organizations, formed and lobbied their respective state and local governments as well as the federal government to respond to the needs of battered women, from arrest and prosecution of their batterers to funding for a wide range of social services.[101]

At the same time, litigation challenging official police policies was occurring, with police departments in Oakland, California and New York City ultimately agreeing to change their policies regarding non–arrest in domestic violence cases.[102] On the heels of those lawsuits came a number of events in 1984 that would shape the future of domestic violence policy.

In 1984, a Minneapolis study found that arrest had a deterrent effect on domestic violence offenders.[103] The creators of the study, however, specifically warned against creating national policy until the findings could be replicated in other cities.[104] That same year, in *Thurman v. City of Torrington, Conn*,[105] a highly publicized case, Tracey Thurman was awarded 2.3 million dollars after suing the Torrington, Connecticut police department for its repeated failure to adequately respond to her calls for help, and ultimately, standing by watching as her husband beat and stomped her, causing her permanent paralysis. Fearing huge financial consequences, police departments across the country started to re–evaluate their policies.[106]

Then in 1984 with a conservative family values administration in power, the focus on violence against women moved from a political issue based on male hegemony and women's equality, to a conservative issue of crime control.[107] Citing the Minneapolis study as support, the Attorney

MANDATORY ARREST & PROSECUTION

General's Task Force on Family Violence recommended arrest and criminal prosecution as the preferred method of addressing this crisis.[108] To this day, criminal justice interventions are the primary means of addressing domestic violence, with federal funding conditioned on states instituting pro arrest and prosecution policies.[109]

Yet, some of the subsequent arrest studies funded by the National Institute of Justice in the late 1980s failed to produce the results of the Minneapolis experiment.[110] In fact, three studies—in Milwaukee, Omaha and Charlotte—found that for certain domestic violence offenders, specifically those who were unemployed and without a "stake in conformity," arrest actually caused an escalation in violence.[111] While the subsequent studies called into question the efficacy of mandatory arrest for certain offenders—the very offenders that make up the bulk of the defendants in the criminal justice system—legislatures ignored those findings and continued to pass legislation mandating arrest in cases of domestic violence.[112]

While the replication studies were limited to analyzing the effects of arrest on recidivism rates,[113] subsequent studies looked at the impact of a coordinated community response from arrest, prosecution and batterer intervention programs on recidivism rates. But the results from those studies were mixed at best.[114]

In any event, by the mid 1990s, a coordinated criminal justice response took hold, with prosecutors' offices throughout the country instituting mandatory prosecution policies, also known as "no–drop policies."[115] Some jurisdictions instituted "hard no–drop policies"[116] where charges would proceed regardless of a woman's wishes even if it meant jailing women for contempt of court. Other offices, like mine, developed a more nuanced approach.

From the start, prosecutors encountered resistance from the very women these policies were supposed to benefit. Not all women, it turned out, wanted their batterers arrested or prosecuted, so they refused to cooperate in the criminal prosecution.[117] In response, prosecutors started pursuing criminal cases with other evidence. This policy, known as evidence–based prosecution, has resulted in fundamental disagreements within the battered women's movement. Prosecutors and scholars have justified such policies in order to send a strong message of zero tolerance for domestic violence regardless of a woman's wishes,[118] while opponents have stressed that loss of women's autonomy, a fundamental tenet of the battered women's movement, is too high a price to pay.[119]

As a result, many scholars and activists have called for a paradigm shift that moves away from an over-reliance on the criminal justice system.[120] I, too, believe that criminal prosecution has been a less than perfect solution. In my experience, mandatory policies have not improved the quality of women's lives, especially for poor women of color, or changed cultural attitudes regarding violence against women.[121] Yet, our national policy continues to focus on criminal justice initiatives to the detriment of other reforms.[122] But does this mean that we should abandon mandatory policies altogether as some have suggested?[123]

While there are certainly costs to engaging with the criminal justice system, especially for poor women and women of color,[124] my experience as a prosecutor leads me to believe that abandoning mandatory arrest will take us back to a time when the police failed to treat domestic violence seriously.[125] While the Battered Women's Movement is thirty years strong, there is still a deep cultural bias that violence between intimate partners is a private matter, and that women are shrewish provocateurs of male violence.[126] Moreover, to presume that young officers, unfamiliar with the complexities of intimate abuse, will use their discretion wisely is deeply troubling.[127] Mandatory arrest at least neutralizes the effects of inexperience and bias by requiring officers to take a specific action regardless of their beliefs and inclinations. After all, police officers, as first responders, are a critical step in the process of reaching out to battered women. If they fail to act, many women would have no idea what options are available to them.[128]

Mandatory prosecution, however, is another matter. While prosecution might be appropriate in some cases, it is not the best option in every case. Prosecutors must therefore move away from a one size fits all approach to their cases, to one that accounts for the individual needs of women.[129] In order to do that, prosecutors must incorporate battered women into the decision-making process by listening to their needs, discussing the criminal options, and giving careful consideration to the impact prosecution will have on their lives. That information must then be balanced with the seriousness of the injury, the history of violence and the batterers' criminal record. If we approach each case this way, we might encounter more satisfaction from the women we claim we are trying to help.¹³⁰

No History of Violence
People v. Seth Clark

MOST WOMEN CALL 911 because they want the violence to stop, not because they want their abusers prosecuted. A 911 call, however, can trigger a full-blown response from the system, one that entails arrest and criminal prosecution by the District Attorney's Office. Prosecutors like myself are then left to deal with the fallout when a woman does not wish to go forward with criminal charges.

While my office does not require that every case of domestic violence be prosecuted, I have pursued charges despite the wishes of women because I arrogantly thought that I knew better than they did. That's what happened in this case. I chose to continue with the prosecution despite the wishes of Dawn. I did so because I had a visceral reaction to Seth Clark. But Seth was the father of Dawn's child and she wanted to continue her relationship with him. That should have been a factor I seriously considered. But, it wasn't.

Dawn was twenty-two when I met her. She had a little girl with Seth, and a six-year-old son from a prior relationship. Seth was twenty years her senior and had fourteen children with a number of different women. It was hard not to view him as a predator after learning some facts about him, like the way he entered Dawn into a thong underwear contest, and kept the proceeds when she won.

Dawn wanted Seth to attend a batterers' program believing it would help change his behavior. But I told her otherwise, explaining that the criminal justice system has no magic formula to stop the violence.[131]

NO HISTORY OF VIOLENCE

I have pursued charges despite the wishes of women because I arrogantly thought that I knew better than they did.

Dawn's mother and father came to see me. They wanted to get Dawn away from Seth, and wanted to know what I could do to make that happen. They were concerned parents. Dawn's mother just had a difficult way of showing it.

"His feet were dirty," Dawn's mother said with disgust as she recounted the day Dawn first brought him home. Her anger was palpable. Dawn's father was quiet and soft-spoken. His wife did most of the talking. She kept referring to Seth as a low-life. I tried to warn her about talking that way in front of Dawn, how Dawn would be more likely to stay in the relationship if she continued to belittle Seth. I told her how it would be best if she focused on Dawn's safety rather than on her choices in men. But she didn't listen.

The first time I saw Seth Clark, he was sitting on a bench outside the courtroom in the Criminal Court building. He was wearing a short sleeve silk shirt that hung over his slacks. He was bald. I stood a few feet away, watching him talk to a pretty young woman who was seated beside him. He was charming.

Seth was on trial for assaulting Dawn in December of 2002. His reason for beating her? She had kept him waiting outside in his car for fifteen minutes while she was in her parents' home picking up some things for her kids. Seth let her know how angry he was when they got back home.

"Help me daddy, help me. He's beating me."

"You called your fucking parents?" was the last thing Dawn's father heard before the phone went dead.

By the time Dawn's parents arrived, police cars were blocking the street. "This is a family matter," Seth's mother yelled as she tried to shut the door in the Sergeant's face. Dawn was screaming in the background. That's when one of the officers saw a male hand smack Dawn across the face. The officers pushed past Seth's mother and dragged him out of the apartment. He was arrested for misdemeanor assault; his mother for obstructing justice.

Dawn ran out of the house into her father's arms. Her hair was wild from being pulled. A few days later Dawn and her children went to a domestic violence shelter. About a month later, she came to my office. Dawn did not want to proceed with the criminal prosecution. Instead, she wanted to go to couples counseling and work on her relationship.

Dawn had been leaving messages on my voicemail, wanting to know why I was pursuing criminal charges against her husband if she was not interested in proceeding with the case. "Because he broke the law," I said when she finally reached me.

Hindsight, they say, is 20/20. In time, I would come to see how my decision to prosecute this case was not in Dawn's best interest. I didn't think about the way my actions would affect Dawn's relationship with Seth, or how I would further alienate her from her parents by using them as witnesses.[132] At the time, I just didn't want a smug defendant like Seth to get away with what he had done.

I refused to back down even though Seth's actions barely rose to a crime. Under the law it was merely harassment and carried very little punishment, like many of the eight thousand misdemeanor domestic violence crimes handled by my bureau each year.

I spoke with every officer who responded to Seth's home on the day of the assault. All the officers heard Dawn's cries for help, yet only one officer witnessed her being hit. But given his angle at the door he only saw the hand on her face, not the person who hit her. That was all the evidence I had the day I announced ready for trial.

The trial was held in Criminal Court before Judge Anne Gills. She would decide Seth's fate. Judge Gills was elected to the Civil Court but assigned to the Criminal Court. Judge Gills wore blue latex gloves. I was so distracted by her hands, wondering if she was like Monk, the obsessive–compulsive television detective, or if there was some other reason she wore them. Throughout the trial she had a tight, pinched, sour expression on her face, and was constantly consulting with her law clerk, who sat behind her.

I stood at a podium in the rundown courtroom, asking questions of my three witnesses: Dawn's father, the Sergeant and the arresting officer.

Seth's attorney stood in front of his podium, a few feet away from mine. He kept creeping into my area and staring at me. He was ready for the attack, screaming "objection" before I even finished my questions. Every time he did this, the judge would raise her latex gloved hand, motioning to the witness to remain silent as she contemplated her ruling on the objection.

It took me an hour to present my case. I could tell by the judge's facial expressions that she was troubled by some of the minor inconsistencies between my witnesses, like whether the front gate was open or closed, and what time Dawn's father got there. She would look at her law clerk with one eyebrow raised and an "Ah hah" expression on her face. It didn't matter to the judge that my witnesses were consistent on the most important facts: that Dawn was crying, disheveled, and bruised when she ran screaming out of the house that day.

It was pouring rain when we left the court building. I stood under the awning of the building with the arresting officer and Sergeant waiting for it to stop. "Thanks for fucking lying," Seth said as he walked passed us.

On the following day, Seth came to court wearing a pair of jeans and a button-down shirt that exposed his chest. The judge called me and the defense attorney up to the bench. "Is there any way you can resolve this?" she asked.

"I want him in a batterers' program," I said. I knew it wouldn't change him. There just weren't any other options in terms of punishment, or accountability. "If you have satisfactory progress reports after ten weeks, I'll let you out," she said to Seth. After consulting with his attorney, Seth agreed.

At the time, I felt like I had won, forcing a defendant like Seth Clark into a program where he would have to listen to lectures on power and control for at least ten weeks.

About a month later a warrant was issued for Seth's arrest because he never went to the program. The only recourse I had was to retry him. But given the Judge's reaction the first time around, I knew that it would be futile.

I took all these steps to hold Seth Clark accountable because he was a batterer under arrest. But to what end? What were the benefits of my involvement in Dawn's life? Yes, the police got her out of the apartment safely, but after that, what good came out of this prosecution?

In retrospect, I should not have pursued the criminal charges.¹³³ This was Seth's first arrest, and there was no history of violence so I should have respected Dawn's decision to stay in her relationship. I also should have asked Dawn what she felt she needed to make her situation better. I wish I had left her with the understanding that she could call me if she ever needed help.¹³⁴ Unfortunately, I left her with the sense that I had only made matters worse, and that I could not be trusted.

Moreover, I couldn't provide Dawn with what she really wanted: a safe forum to work on her relationship. In order to address the lack of options for women like Dawn, some domestic violence advocates have supported the use of restorative justice programs in conjunction with the criminal justice system.¹³⁵ These programs claim to offer victims and offenders an opportunity to work together through a "process whereby parties with a stake in a specific offense collectively resolve how to deal with the aftermath of the offense and its implications for the future."¹³⁶

While I question whether such programs can change the dynamics of an abusive relationship, I do think we need more options for women who want to address the violence in their relationships.¹³⁷

Restorative justice programs are gaining traction in communities across the United States with reports of success in some cases.¹³⁸ Giving Dawn the option of entering such a program might have helped her in her relationship, or at least let her feel that the system was responsive to her needs. By handling the case the way I did, I did the exact opposite.

What's worse is that I had been a domestic violence prosecutor for eight years when I pursued this case. At the time, I truly believed that I was "doing the right thing."¹³⁹ It was only after I started my research for this book that I began to see things differently. Prior to that, I routinely dismissed any criticism of my work, believing that opponents just "didn't get it."

Without proper education and training, prosecutors like me may continue to act inappropriately without even realizing it. After all, not every prosecutor who handles domestic violence cases has a background in feminist theory. Assistants are often rotated into a domestic violence unit with no history or context for understanding the work that they are doing.

As a result, many prosecutor's offices throughout the United States have developed thought provoking training exercises for newly assigned

Without proper education and training, prosecutors like me may continue to act inappropriately without even realizing it. After all, not every prosecutor who handles domestic violence cases has a background in feminist theory. Assistants are often rotated into a domestic violence unit with no history or context for understanding the work that they are doing.

assistants.[140] Some of the exercises require assistants to read books by domestic violence activists like Anne Jones,[141] and then debate the issues raised in the books. Other exercises place the prosecutor in the very crisis situation that battered women find themselves in. The exercises are developed in such a way that what appears at first blush to be an easy quick–fix solution, like leaving the relationship, is revealed to be much more complicated. The easy fix may have multiple and sometimes devastating consequences. The point of the exercises is to get prosecutors to be more sensitive and less judgmental, and to understand the complexities underlying battered women's choices.

Hopefully, training exercises like these will help prosecutors engage in a more nuanced approach to their cases instead of a one size fits all approach, like I engaged in when I prosecuted Seth Clark.

A History of Violence
People v. Paul Gordon

EAST FLATBUSH, BROOKLYN has one of the highest reported rates of domestic violence in New York City. In the heart of this largely Caribbean–American community lies a housing development containing close to 3,000 apartments. The tenants are mostly poor and black. The complex used to be run by slumlords who refused to fix the garbage compactors, door locks or window locks. As the rats roamed through the buildings, the owners cashed the government checks that were generously doled out for housing the city's less fortunate.

This was the place Linda called home. I first met Linda in the summer of 2001, a few days after her boyfriend had been arrested. This was his third arrest for domestic violence against Linda but it was the first time she had come to my office. She was only twenty-one. Linda was extremely polite, calling me Ms. Kaminsky before answering any of my questions. "Call me Michelle," I said repeatedly, but she never did. I was immediately taken by Linda. She was so spirited and had such high hopes for a better life.

Linda met Paul when she was fifteen. Three months after meeting, she was pregnant. As a result, her mother kicked her out. With nowhere else to go she moved in with Paul. When he started to beat her, she fled to a domestic violence shelter.

The waiting room in my bureau is filled with young, poor, minority single mothers just like Linda. Most have their first child in their teens,

A HISTORY OF VIOLENCE

I took for granted the basic necessities of food, clothing, shelter, and education. Linda did not. But she never looked for pity.

and by their mid-twenties, have had four to five children with different men. Most of these men have criminal records.

Whenever Linda would come to my office she would tell me that she was going to get a better job so that she could get out of the projects and give her daughter, Tracey, a better life. She became extremely animated, as if she could actually feel it happening. I couldn't help but think about my own life and how easy I had it growing up. I took for granted the basic necessities of food, clothing, shelter, and education. Linda did not. But she never looked for pity.

Linda moved from the Bronx to Brooklyn, hoping that a change of location would help her get her life on track and help her get away from Paul. But her minimum wage job at McDonald's, and her public assistance benefits, were scarcely enough to enable her to rise out of poverty or escape from Paul. With no family support, and no extra cash to hire someone, Linda was often forced to rely on Paul to baby-sit.[142]

Paul only made matters worse. Soon after Linda moved to Brooklyn, Paul found another girlfriend, who lived in the apartment directly above Linda's. He would have sex upstairs and then come down to Linda's expecting to spend the night with her. Linda would later explain to a jury how upset she was by Paul's behavior, but that she couldn't stop him because when she would refuse to let him in, Paul would break into her apartment through the fire escape window.

Every so often, Linda would reach her breaking point and call the police. But every time he was arrested, Linda never pursued the criminal charges. "They make you sit there all these hours, I don't want to sit there any more because I have done this over and over and over and they keep letting him out," she claimed. Ironically, the reason Paul was always let out of jail was because Linda never followed through with the criminal prosecution.[143]

Linda had once told me that she didn't want to be like those people in the projects who talk about getting out, yet spend their whole lives there. She did everything she could to get out. That included enrolling in a local technical school to learn a trade. The day before her graduation she came to my office beaming with delight.

But no matter how hard she tried to better her circumstances, Paul kept showing up and Linda kept taking him back, believing that things would be different. But they never were. Soon after her course began, Paul dragged Linda up to the roof of her building where he forced her to perform oral sex on him. He was screaming that he wanted to die, alternating between threatening to jump and begging Linda to kill him.

Paul had unlimited access to Linda's apartment since he had stolen her house keys and broken her window locks. When Linda tried to get new locks, the management company would only change the bottom lock, expecting Linda to pay for a new dead bolt, a security measure she could hardly afford. The reality was if you couldn't afford security, then you couldn't have it.

One evening Linda left for school at around five. When she returned, she couldn't open her door because Paul was inside the apartment and had locked the dead bolt. Linda ran down three flights onto the street and flagged down a passing patrol car. Out of breath and crying, Linda waved a bundle of domestic incident reports at the officers, reports that had been taken over the last few days.[144] She frantically told them that her baby's father was inside her apartment and that he didn't belong there and that she wanted him arrested.

The police kicked down her door and searched for Paul with their weapons drawn. They looked in every room, in every closet, underneath the beds and behind the shower curtain, but they didn't find him. Knowing that he had to be there, Linda tore up the apartment, desperate to find him before the police left. The Sergeant later told me that at that point he thought she was delusional. He was immediately proven wrong. "He's in the mattress, he's in the mattress," Linda screamed. Paul was hiding between the wooden slats of the boxspring with a boxcutter by his side, waiting for the police to leave, waiting to be alone with Linda.

Linda went to the local precinct that night and sat down on a seat anchored to the wall as the arresting officer finished his paperwork. I was always struck by the contrast between the routine business of the police precinct and the incredible anxiety of the victims. There was a monotony to the endless ring of the switchboard, the clicking of the typewriters, and the comings and goings of the various police personnel, while the victims, whose lives had been turned upside down, sat waiting not knowing what would happen next.

Paul was twenty-six when I first saw him in court. He was skinny and short and looked like a gawky teenager, rather than a violent individual. Tracey looked just like him.

That night he was charged with burglary for breaking into Linda's home. Close to twenty-four hours after his arrest, he was brought before a judge who set bail at $ 25,000. With no friends or family to put up the money, Paul was sent to Rikers Island Correctional Facility to await trial. Linda was finally ready to proceed with the prosecution. She even agreed to see a therapist on staff with the district attorney's office and attended a few counseling sessions. But her cooperation was short lived. By November, Linda showed up at Paul's court appearance, handing a letter to the judge where she said it was all a big misunderstanding and that she wanted to drop charges.

When I questioned Linda as to why she wrote the letter, she told me that she felt bad that her kid's father was in jail, that she loved him and that she did not want to see him in trouble. She also told me that Paul's brother had called her and asked, "How can you put your kid's father in jail? Write a letter to the judge and tell the judge that the D.A. coerced you into cooperating."

Linda's letter was not unusual. Many women feel guilty about calling the police once the violence has stopped. This often results in letters just like Linda's.[145] While I knew Linda had lied in the letter, I would still have to convince a jury of that.

Linda was visiting Paul in jail, talking to him on the phone and depositing money into his commissary account so he could buy snacks and cigarettes. To see how often they were talking, I combed through his inmate phone records, highlighting every call to Linda. By the time I finished, most of the pages were neon yellow; Paul had called Linda 500 times in five months.

I didn't want to upset Linda, so I waited until the trial date approached before telling her that she would have to testify. By that time her telephone had been disconnected because she couldn't afford the bills.

It was a sweltering hot day in the beginning of June when I went out to Linda's apartment, hoping to track her down. The courtyard outside her building was made of asphalt with some basketball hoops that hung off the ten-foot high chain link fence that surrounded the complex. Tenants were sitting outside on folding chairs trying to cool down as some children amused themselves by jumping up and down on a bunch of old dirty discarded mattresses that were lying in the middle of the courtyard. The air inside the building was stifling and the elevator floor was wet with urine.

Linda looked annoyed when she opened her front door. She told me that she did not want to testify against Paul, and that she was in a rush because she had to be at work in an hour. I tried to speak to Linda about the case as she ironed her work uniform but she was too distracted to pay attention. I felt doomed. This case was scheduled for trial in a few short weeks and my key witness refused to talk to me.

I could hear Tracey sobbing for her daddy from the back bedroom. When I went over to her, she was huddled in the corner of the room with tears streaming down her face, clutching an oversized teddy bear. I wanted to comfort her, to make it better, to give her back her father. But her father was physically and sexually assaulting her mother. How could I ignore that reality?[146]

After talking for 20 minutes, Linda said she had to go and jumped in the shower. I waited in the courtyard as Linda went from one building to the next, looking for some neighbor to watch Tracey because she could not afford to pay a babysitter. When she finally found one, I took her to work.

In light of Linda's history of ignoring subpoenas, the trial judge, at my request, issued a warrant for her arrest on the day she was scheduled to testify. Forcing this woman into a situation she had tried so hard to avoid left me with a sinking feeling in the pit of my stomach. But I was a prosecutor and Paul was under arrest.

At seven a.m., two Detectives knocked on Linda's door, roused her out of bed and brought her and her daughter to the District Attorney's Office. Linda was extremely upset when she came to my office, wanting to know why she had to testify. I explained to her that Paul was unwilling to plead guilty to any charge, including a misdemeanor, unless he was released from jail the very same day. The judge, however, would not release him until a sentencing report was completed and that would take ten days.

Paul was risking going to prison for a couple of years just because he didn't want to wait another ten days in jail. When Linda heard this—that Paul was unwilling to do anything to help himself—she got angry. And when Linda realized that I had done everything possible to keep her from testifying—short of dismissing the case—she finally agreed to speak with me.

Linda was twenty-two years old when the case came to trial. For a good part of her testimony, she had her head down on the witness stand. At times her voice was barely audible. It was clear to all that she did not want to be there. There were even times during her testimony that Linda glanced over to Paul and smiled. At one point, during a break in the proceedings, Linda mouthed to Paul "stupid, stupid," referring to his refusal to take a misdemeanor plea.

In order to prove all the charges, Linda had to testify in detail about all the times he forced her to have sex. That meant that she had to tell twelve strangers, a judge and courtroom personnel how the father of her child repeatedly hit her, choked her and pulled her hair until she performed oral or vaginal sex. The horror of her experience was lost in the clinical nature of the proceedings. "Listen we have to hear from you, so I'll ask you in a more general way. How did this occur; just describe the events as briefly and succinctly, but with as much detail as you can," the judge said. But Linda wouldn't. After barely testifying to two incidents, she stated, "I don't want to talk about it, Ms. Kaminsky."

It was close to five p.m. when I finished my questioning. The judge let the jury go for the day, informing Linda that she would have to come back the following morning. Tears fell from her eyes. The judge responded with compassion. "No one intends to make you cry. I think just talking about the event is making you cry, is that correct, just talking about it." Linda shook her head in agreement as the tears rolled down her face. "No one will be harsh with you. No one is picking on you. We all just want to know what happened," the judge kindly said.

The following day Linda was in much better spirits. I think she had gotten over her fear, and that enabled her personality to shine through when she answered the defense attorney's questions on cross–examination. When he tried to imply that Linda was high on drugs because her head was down on the witness stand during my questioning, Linda responded with irony, "Maybe I was praying, praying that it would be over soon."

Unable to rattle Linda or score any points with the jury, the attorney moved on to another line of questioning, confronting Linda with a sexually explicit letter that she had written to Paul while he was in jail, in which she expressed her love for him and described all the sexual acts she wanted to perform with him.

Paul was all excited, moving about in his seat giggling as his attorney questioned Linda. I had witnessed this so many times, defendants getting a thrill at the expense of their victims.

In the end, Linda came off as a woman who was just trying to get by in life, a woman struggling to earn a living so she could provide for herself and her daughter. And she was doing this while also contending with an abusive boyfriend, a man who was not just her batterer, but who was also her lover and the father of her child.

In keeping with her conflicting feelings, Linda made one last effort to protect Paul, testifying that Paul was only removing his clothes from her apartment the night he was found wedged in the box spring of her bed. This gave him a legitimate reason to be inside her apartment, foreclosing a conviction for burglary. The jury managed to sift through the confusing, and at times conflicting testimony, and after a few hours of deliberation, settled on a conviction for Criminal Contempt in the First Degree for hitting her while an order of protection was in effect.

From a prosecutorial perspective, justice was achieved. Paul Gordon was convicted of a felony offense and held accountable for his actions. He was sentenced to one to three years' incarceration, denied parole and held by the parole board for another year.

About a year later, Linda contacted me out of the blue. She was moving to another state and needed a letter to help obtain housing. She

> *While activists opposed to mandatory policies have argued that women should ultimately decide whether or not to go forward with a criminal case, even if the choice can lead to further violence, I don't believe this is a workable solution in all cases.*

sounded well and informed me that she had found a wonderful man and that they were planning on getting married. I asked her to stop by so we could talk. I had thought about her often during that year. She told me she would come by the following day, but she never did.

Just like Dawn from the previous chapter, Linda did not want her abuser prosecuted. She too was tied to him by a child and that emotional connection had an impact on her choice. The critical distinction between this case and Dawn's, however, was the history of violence and the severity of the crime. Paul had a history of beating and threatening Linda; Seth did not. Paul's current crime was a felony; Seth's was not.[147]

I look back at this case and believe that I "did the right thing."[148] I pursued the matter because of the seriousness of the charges and because there were no alternatives. In the world of the criminal justice system, there were merely three options: plea, trial or dismissal. I offered a plea but Paul refused. I couldn't dismiss because Paul had a history of violence. So I was left with only one other choice, and that was trial.

While activists opposed to mandatory policies have argued that women should ultimately decide whether or not to go forward with a criminal case, even if the choice can lead to further violence,[149] I don't believe this is a workable solution in all cases.

Linda, like many women, was continuously reaching out to the police for help because she wanted the violence to stop. But Paul refused to leave Linda alone. In fact, each time he was released from jail the abuse escalated. To argue the state should back off in such circumstances is not realistic.

For those critics of mandatory policies who say the state demeans women and merely replaces the batterer by going forward with charges, I say this analysis simplifies a very complex situation. [150] In the first place, I never saw Linda as powerless and unable to act in her own best interest, and thus in need of the power of the state to make the right decision for her. I understood that she wanted the violence to end, but didn't want to take part in the process. Unfortunately, it was a Catch–22 situation that the criminal justice system could not entirely resolve.

Moreover, I tried to respect Linda's desire not to be involved in the process, but Paul refused to take any responsibility. Should I have dismissed the case and ceded all power to Paul, the very person who was beating Linda? As a society, should we give batterers that kind of power? The answer for me is a resounding no.

Clearly, there is an inherent tension between the very function of the criminal justice system and the desires of many women. While it's a tension that can't be resolved, we as prosecutors can approach our cases with more sensitivity to a woman's particular needs. Yet, batterers like Paul often hijack our ability to do so. This is a major obstacle to the satisfactory resolution of these cases and one that the system must more effectively address.[151]

Furthermore, Linda's options were limited by the fact that she had no social support and limited economic opportunities. This made her more dependent on the criminal justice system to stop the violence. This is another obstacle in the lives of many battered women. However, it is an obstacle that can't be addressed by the criminal justice system; it must be addressed by domestic violence policy makers. [152]

Finally, I don't think Linda was disempowered by the system. On the contrary, I think Linda was empowered when she heard that I had done everything to keep her from testifying but that Paul refused to cooperate in that process. In fact, that's when Linda got fed up and agreed to testify. And ultimately Linda was the one who controlled what she told the court and jury about what was done to her. She had the final say and no one could force her to say more than she was willing to.

3

Obstacles to Holding Offenders Accountable: Working Within the Adversarial System

THE VIOLENCE AGAINST WOMEN ACT of 1994 was a monumental piece of legislation. After years of lobbying by battered women's advocates, Congress finally acknowledged the devastating impact domestic violence has on women, and the collateral consequences it has on the nation.[153] According to the Centers for Disease Control (CDC), each year approximately five million women are victims of domestic violence.[154] Data from the CDC further reveals that domestic violence costs this country over eight billion dollars a year in health care and lost productivity.[155]

The Act, and its subsequent reauthorizations, encouraged a strong law enforcement response by funding state criminal justice initiatives.[156] Since its passage, the trend in the United States has been to address domestic violence through the criminal justice system. This is a complicated task given the adversarial nature of the system. While prosecutors are charged with bringing about this goal, defense attorneys have a different mandate, one that requires them to do everything possible to get their clients out of trouble. These opposing objectives can be played out before judges who lack the temperament and insight to preside over domestic violence cases.

In our quest to hold batterers accountable, prosecutors are limited by the evidence in the case, and legal principles which can benefit the accused. Women who are not ready to pursue criminal charges, or who suffer from mental illness and substance abuse issues can further complicate matters.

Then there is the matter of deterrence. In the criminal justice system punishment is meted out in the form of probation, jail or prison. Yet, criminals in general, and batterers in particular, are often undeterred by these consequences.[157]

While policy makers hoped that a strong law enforcement response would cause a reduction in domestic violence, the reality of the situation has proven otherwise. The number of domestic violence cases in Brooklyn has remained constant during my fifteen years in the Domestic Violence Bureau, hovering around eight thousand a year. Batterers continue to find ways to use the adversarial system to their advantage by manipulating and exploiting their victims' fears and financial, emotional and family issues. As a result, many women do not want to follow through with criminal charges. Most of the time, prosecutors are unable to prove the criminal charges without a woman's testimony. Rather than deter batterers and reduce domestic violence, this emboldens them to commit further acts of violence. Many batterers, in fact, are repeat offenders; they come in and out of the criminal justice system, facing minimal consequences for their criminal behavior.

In order to reverse this course, law makers, policy makers and the judiciary need to level the playing field. Prosecutors need effective laws and resources to hold batterers accountable. Law makers, policy makers and the judiciary need to understand that evidentiary rules that exclude prior acts of domestic violence undermine offender accountability; that bail determinations that fail to account for dangerousness undermine offender accountability; that failure to track recidivist batterers through global positioning system (GPS) devices undermine offender accountability; that batterers' constitutional rights are not absolute; that failure to screen and monitor judges presiding over domestic violence cases undermines offender accountability; that working with high risk victims of domestic violence requires multidisciplinary teams; and that failure to adequately fund social service programs leaves victims of domestic violence extremely vulnerable.

The following three cases illustrate the shortcomings of the current system, and how the case outcomes could have been different if these reforms were in place.

Legal Principles & Deterrence
People v. Charles Higgins

On April 14, 1999, Charles Higgins was sentenced to serve three years at Gowanda Correctional Facility near the Canadian border. That sentence was the result of breaking into his girlfriend's apartment and choking her when she tried to run. "You cunt. You bitch. You're gonna die," he screamed before the cops hauled him away.

"He was like an animal. I thought he was going to kill me," Beth would later say when recounting the events of that night.

It was June of 1998 when I first met Beth O'Reilly. She was a pretty, petite blonde with blue eyes. She was only twenty-three. Beth was so quiet sitting in that chair across from my desk. She would barely respond to my questions. I never got an adequate explanation as to why she moved out of her parents' home when she was merely fifteen years-old and moved in with her eighteen year-old girlfriend who was dating Charles Higgins.

Beth described her first sexual encounter with Charles. "I was laying in bed and Charles came in and got on top of me, pulled down my underwear and raped me." Higgins was 6'4, 190 pounds. He was twice her size.

"Did you scream for your friend?" I asked.

"No. I just went numb," she said.

Over the next year, Charles made a habit of climbing into Beth's bed.

Beth eventually confided in her older sister, who in turn told their parents. The very same parents, who Beth had fled from as a teenager, went straight to the police. And those very same parents would spend the next decade of their lives trying to help their daughter.

Higgins was arrested in April of 1991 when Beth was seventeen. Since Higgins never used "force," i.e., no threats or physical violence, against Beth, he was only charged with sexual misconduct, a misdemeanor offense. About a year later, he was sentenced to three years' probation and the court issued a three-year order of protection prohibiting him from having any contact with Beth.

Beth, however, was not ready to leave Higgins, and the two moved in together.

"Why did you get back with him?" I asked years later.

"Because he told me that he loved me," she said.

"Ugly bitch." "Fucking piece of shit." "No one will every want you," he would scream. That was one of his many ways of degrading her. Higgins was like many of the men I prosecuted. The way they needed to break their victims down, needing them to believe that without them they were nothing. It was the same litany I heard over and over again.

Despite the abuse, Beth managed to hold a full time job as a clerk in an office. She even tried to maintain her friendships. But Higgins tried to control every aspect of her life, demanding that she come straight home after work. "What happened if you didn't do what he wanted?"

"He would choke me until I lost consciousness," she said.

After three years of living this way, Beth moved in with a girlfriend.

"I'll never do it again. I love you," Charles pleaded as the tears fell from his eyes.

"Why did you go back?" I asked.

"Because I thought he would change," she said.

"I'll never do it again" lasted for a mere three days. Yet, it took Beth another year before she left him again. This time she moved in with her older sister.

The more Beth tried to assert her independence, the more violent Higgins became. One night, as Beth was walking home, Higgins approached her on the street and pointed a gun at her. "The bullets have your name on it," he warned before walking away. A few weeks later Higgins threw a bottle at her as she walked down the street. "Close your window tonight bitch I'm gonna break it and your father's," he screamed.

LEGAL PRINCIPLES & DETERRENCE

But nothing could deter Higgins: not the police, not the courts, not an order of protection, not the threat of jail.

Fearing for her safety, Beth filed a police report. But nothing could deter Higgins: not the police, not the courts, not an order of protection, not the threat of jail. He was arrested so many times that he was on a first name basis with the detectives at the local precinct.

Higgins' last act against Beth would land him in an upstate penitentiary. It was the night of June 14, 1998 when he broke into Beth's apartment, threw her to the floor, kicked her in the head, and expressed his love as he wrapped his hands around her neck and strangled her. As the police dragged him out in handcuffs, he was screaming, "Beth I'm going to kill you."

Higgins was charged with Burglary in the First Degree.[158] Since he was unable to come up with $ 8,000 in bail, Higgins awaited trial at Rikers Island. Shortly after Beth met with me, she wrote two letters to the court, informing the judge that she wanted to drop all charges against Higgins because they had worked out their problems.

A few weeks later Beth came to my office, letting me know that she'd never testify against him.

"Why not?" I asked.

"Because I love him, and no one, not the police, not the district attorney's office, and not an order of protection, can ever protect me from him."

Since I couldn't prove the charges without Beth's cooperation, I offered Higgins a plea. That's how he ended up at Gowanda. And that's how Beth received a six-year full order of protection that prohibited him from contacting her directly or indirectly through her friends or family.

It was June of 2001 when Higgins was released from prison. He served a little over two years on a three-year sentence. Disregarding the full order of protection, he went looking for Beth weeks after he was released. This time he couldn't find her because she had moved away. Now her family became his focus.

Phyllis and Bob O'Reilly came to my office shortly after Higgins was released. Phyllis brought a large framed photograph of Beth smiling in her graduation gown. Her parents refused to tell me where she was, believing it was the only way to protect her.

A few weeks later I received a call from Phyllis. She was crying. "Ms. Kaminsky, it's Phyllis O'Reilly. I've been sleeping in my car because Charles slashed my tires and broke my car window."

"Did you see him do it?" I asked.

"No, but I know it's him," she said.

"Why are you sleeping in your car?" I asked.

"Because I need my car. We can't afford to keep changing the tires and fixing the windshield. If I stay in the car maybe I can catch him," she said.

Higgins was eventually arrested for calling the O'Reillys looking for Beth, and was sentenced to probation.

"I love Beth and I want to marry her," he told the probation officer at their first meeting.

The judge lost his temper when he heard about Higgins' declaration of love.

"If you screw up, I tell you now, you will get a year in jail. And I want you to stay out of these people's lives," the judge yelled.

But Higgins continued to terrorize the O'Reillys.

"Hey, Samantha, where's Beth?" Higgins asked Beth's eleven-year-old niece, before planting a kiss on the frightened little girl's cheek.

"Don't tell your grandmother you saw me," he warned before walking away.

Samantha came to my office with her grandmother a few days after Higgins was arrested for violating the order of protection. She had an angelic face with soft blue eyes and straight long blonde hair.

About a week later she sent me a drawing. There I was in my office sitting at my desk with Samantha seated across from me. On another sheet of paper she drew a heart and wrote the following note inside:

You were so nice to me, kind and patient.

You did not yell at me for taking my time.

You knew how scared I was. I'm glad it's over.

Roses are red,

Violets are blue,

Michelle Kaminsky is a nice name,
For such a wonderful person like
You!
And this heart is especially for you!!!!

Samantha should have been playing with her friends. Instead, she was making trips to the District Attorney's Office.

It's exasperating the way men like Higgins constantly beat the system. Did it really matter that he was indicted by a grand jury and violated by probation? He still managed to make bail. And within a few short days, he once again violated the order of protection.

Higgins was rumored to be a neighborhood drug dealer, using young teenagers to sell his product. They were with him the day Higgins rode his bicycle down Samantha's street, in direct violation of the order of protection. It was a cat and mouse game, with Higgins baiting everyone, from the O'Reillys to the police. This time, Higgins was arrested on felony charges and brought back before the felony domestic violence judge, the same judge that sentenced him to prison in 1998. This time the judge refused to set bail. Higgins was sent to Rikers Island Correctional Facility.

I remember the day he came before the judge. He was so gangly and had a buzz cut that exposed his long skinny neck tattooed with Chinese letters. He had a perpetual smirk on his face. It stayed there even as the judge warned him about violating the order of protection. A bunch of his teenage buddies were in the courtroom showing their support. Higgins kept turning around exchanging laughs with them.

Samantha's grandparents opposed any plea offer to Higgins, confident that a jury would convict him based solely on Samantha's testimony. I also naively believed that Samantha would win over the jury. My animosity towards Higgins cost me my perspective.

At trial, Higgins received all the benefits of the law, including a favorable ruling from the judge which precluded the jury from hearing about his history with the O'Reilly family. The judge was following established legal principles that protect the accused from their own criminal histories, lest the jury should convict because of that history rather than the evidence in the case.[159] All they learned was that Beth was Samantha's aunt, that she had been in an "abusive" relationship with Higgins, and that there was an order of protection ordering him to stay away from Beth and her family.

It was the jury that would decide Higgins' guilt or innocence. My goal was to find twelve men and women who could rely solely on an eleven–year–old witness. But there is no science to selecting such a jury, and no way of knowing if they were being truthful when answering my questions. The judge allowed me fifteen minutes of questioning for every group of sixteen prospective jurors. That came out to approximately one minute per person. One minute to find out about their beliefs and prejudices. One minute to find out if they would be "right" for the case.

I specifically questioned them about their ability to believe a child witness and their ability to convict solely on the testimony of a child. "Oh yes, we can do that," they all assured me. Only one juror was able to keep that promise. After a full day of holding out, that one juror finally acquiesced and went along with the other 11, acquitting Charles Higgins of all charges.

I waited in the lobby of the courthouse to speak with them. "How come you didn't convict?" I asked.

"Well we believed Samantha, but we needed more than just her," they said.

While I was angry at their decision, I realized it was inevitable given how much was kept from them. They had no context for understanding what Higgins was doing to Samantha and her family. They had no idea that he had been terrorizing them for over a decade. And without that context, they were loathe to convict.

It's been years since I've heard from the O'Reillys. But I recently heard from Higgins' new girlfriend and mother of his infant son. He was now doing to her exactly what he had done to Beth.

This is a common story: offenders, like Higgins, never really stopping their abuse, just merely moving on to their next victim. The criminal justice response in this case, like so many, was nothing more than a band–aid measure. But with some statutory and policy reforms like admission of prior acts of domestic violence, use of the doctrine of forfeiture by wrongdoing as discussed below, and monitoring through GPS, the criminal justice system can turn the tables on batterers like Higgins, and hold them accountable once and for all.

Sociologist and battered women's expert Evan Stark, has described the ongoing nature of a batterer's abuse as "coercive control," emphasizing the batterer's desire to dominate his victim.[160] Yet, the crime for which Higgins was charged, namely criminal contempt for violating the order of protection, captured neither the true nature of his abuse, nor his motivation.[161] The result was that the jury was presented with a distorted version of events disconnected from the reality of Higgins' criminal conduct.

Recognizing this failure, Evan Stark, as well as some legal scholars, have advocated for legislation criminalizing a batterer's intent to gain power and control over their victims by engaging in a course of conduct.[162] While such legislation would account for the true nature of a batterer's behavior, I'm not sure it will change three recurring and problematic aspects of domestic violence prosecutions: the vast majority of women don't want to proceed with criminal charges[163]; batterers coerce victims out of cooperating with the prosecution [164]; and juries tend to focus on the reasons why women stay in the relationship rather than the batterer's criminal conduct. [165]

In my experience, the substance of the criminal charge was never a factor in a woman's decision not to go forward. Rather, concerns over safety, finances, child care, and love for their batterers were.[166] There is no reason to believe that different legislation will change these circumstances.

Moreover, power and control are nebulous concepts. In order to make out these criminal elements at trial, prosecutors may have to rely on expert testimony. My concern is that expert testimony will exacerbate the problem of victim blaming as defense counsel, during cross–examination, will undoubtedly focus on the victim's behavior, arguing that she was complicit in the abuse, thus shifting the focus away from the batterer's criminal conduct.[167]

While current criminal laws are problematic, we can certainly use them more effectively. We should be doing everything possible to hold batterers responsible when they coerce their victims out of cooperating in the criminal proceedings, a situation rampant in domestic violence prosecutions. [168]

The United States Supreme Court has addressed this phenomenon in two recent cases.[169] In both decisions, the Court discussed the common law doctrine of forfeiture by wrongdoing. This doctrine holds that

The doctrine of forfeiture by wrongdoing can change the landscape of domestic violence prosecutions and lead to a paradigm shift.

a defendant's constitutional right of confrontation[170] is not absolute and can be extinguished if a defendant engages in conduct designed to procure a witness's absence at trial. Thus, if a batterer engages in misconduct in order to keep his victim from testifying at trial, he forfeits his right of confrontation, and his right to object to the admission of hearsay testimony.[171]

Use of this doctrine would have enabled me to go forward with the original felony case against Higgins for burglarizing and assaulting Beth. By using Higgins' prior history of physical abuse against Beth, his threats to kill her at the time he was taken away by the police and any post arrest contact with her, I would have shown that Higgins was directly responsible for Beth's refusal to testify at trial.[172]

After all, Beth's conflicting feelings of love and fear were the direct result of Higgins' behavior towards her. He beat her, threatened her, micro-managed her life, and then begged for forgiveness, professing his love and inability to live without her.[173]

Higgins engaged in this behavior to maintain control over Beth and keep her in a battering relationship.[174] If I was successful, then I would have been able to use any reliable out of court hearsay statements made by Beth against Higgins at trial. This powerful evidence could have led to a top count conviction, or enabled me, during plea negotiations, to negotiate for a significant prison sentence.[175]

The doctrine of forfeiture by wrongdoing can change the landscape of domestic violence prosecutions and lead to a paradigm shift. The burden of holding a recidivist batterer responsible for his conduct would be taken off of the victim and shifted to the perpetrator, and his post-arrest behavior. This would lead to a change in the nature of the discourse between prosecutors, the defense bar and the court. The conversation would no longer be about the victim not wanting to cooperate and the need to plead out or dismiss the criminal case, but about the batterers' post–arrest conduct and how this behavior has impacted the victim's ability to cooperate with the prosecution.

Furthermore, Higgins' post–release behavior underscores the need for 24/7 monitoring of recidivist batterers with GPS devices.[176] Unfortunately, at the time Higgins was sentenced, the law did not provide for post–release supervision of prisoners serving determinate sentences. However, New York has since enacted such legislation.[177] Assuming Higgins was on post–release supervision, and as a condition of his release he was monitored by a GPS device, I wonder whether he would have continued to violate the order knowing that a computer was recording his every move.[178]

While GPS is expensive because of the manpower required for the 24/7 monitoring, and is not foolproof, it just might be the additional tool needed to help deter recidivist batterers.[179] These devices can be programmed to include exclusion zones, areas where batterers are forbidden to enter.[180] Sixteen states, through legislation, now provide for GPS monitoring of domestic violence offenders either as a condition of pre–trial or post–conviction supervision.[181] If a batterer crossed into the exclusion zone, an alarm would go off to the monitoring agency, who would in turn notify the police.[182] In this case, Beth's home as well as the home of her parents, and any places they frequented, could have been programmed into the device and made part of the exclusion zone. Also, Beth and her parents could have been alerted if Higgins crossed into the excluded areas.[183] GPS provides irrefutable evidence, separate and apart from the victim, that the batterer has violated the order of protection. This is exactly what is needed given how juries are reluctant to convict on witness testimony alone.

Finally, if Higgins' entire history of abuse came out at trial, Higgins would probably still be in jail. But instead, Higgins was able to hide behind evidentiary principles that exclude this information at trial.[184] The vast majority of states allow the admission of prior acts of violence only for the limited purpose of proving a matter that the defendant has put in issue like the identity of the offender, whether the offender had the necessary criminal intent, the offender's motive or to challenge the offender's claim that he merely acted in self-defense.[185]

To further compound matters, defense counsel engaged in an unfair and misleading cross-examination of Samantha by questioning her about incidents that occurred when she was six years-old, incidents for which she had no memory. Defense counsel used this to his advantage in summation, arguing that Samantha was untrustworthy because she couldn't remember events when she was six, yet conveniently remembered events the day Higgins violated the order of protection. The law should not give a batterer the sword of cross-examination and at the very same time a shield excluding prior acts of domestic violence. To do otherwise leads to a gross miscarriage of justice with men like Higgins getting away with their crimes.

States need to amend their evidentiary codes to allow for the admission of prior acts of domestic violence.[186] Imagine if the jury, in addition to hearing Samantha's testimony, heard about Higgins' entire history of abuse with Beth, putting the violation of the order of protection in its proper context. They would have known about a history of abuse dating back ten years, culminating in a felony conviction where Higgins admitted his guilt in a plea allocution and served two years in prison. Then they would have understood that as soon as Higgins got out of prison he went looking for Beth, and when he couldn't find her, he targeted her immediate family, letting them know that no one could stop him. That's what this case was about. Yet, the jury never understood because the law protected Higgins from his own criminality.[187]

Judges & Defense Attorneys:
People v. Thomas Cross

THE DISTRICT ATTORNEY'S Office occupies ten floors of a high rise glass tower in the heart of downtown Brooklyn, right at the foot of the Brooklyn Bridge. The Domestic Violence Bureau is on the fifteenth floor, with offices on the perimeter and a series of cubicles in the center, forming a maze—like structure.

At 9:00 a.m., women of all ages and color get off the elevator and head to the waiting room. At times it resembles an emergency room as women with black eyes sit next to women with broken bones. A few feet away their children play in the brightly decorated playroom where teddy bears and games fill the shelves.

That's the playroom where Jennifer's daughter was pretending to teach her make—believe students as Jennifer and I figured out what to do next. Thomas had been bombarding her with phone calls, threatening to hurt her if she didn't get back with him.

Thomas was one of my repeat offenders. A few years prior I had prosecuted him for assaulting another girlfriend. Now he was back again for assaulting Jennifer, his former high school girlfriend. Thomas had fourteen misdemeanor convictions gracing his rap sheet. Standing close to 5'5", Thomas had the habit of jerking his shoulder forward while simultaneously lifting one nostril upward like a mobster.

Thomas had an unusual way of expressing his love. He liked to call Jennifer "cunt" rather than her name. When he needed to show his

Thomas had an unusual way of expressing his love. He liked to call Jennifer "cunt" rather than her name. When he needed to show his feelings, he would pull out chunks of her hair. And when Jennifer failed to perform oral sex to his liking, he would spit in her face.

feelings, he would pull out chunks of her hair. And when Jennifer failed to perform oral sex to his liking, he would spit in her face.

Every so often Jennifer would reach her breaking point and either call me or the police. "Ms. Kaminsky, it's Jennifer Fine. He won't leave me alone. He keeps calling. I got to be at work. They are going to fire me."

Inevitably, the conversations turned to money, to her inability to make the rent, or pay the bills, and to the fact that Thomas' abuse was interfering with her ability to keep her job.

Jennifer always called me a few weeks after Thomas' arrest, informing me that they had worked out their problems and that she was no longer interested in pursuing the criminal case or the order of protection.

"Our families are friends and the order of protection will only interfere with that," Jennifer would say.

"Does your mother know what he has been doing to you?" I asked.

"Yes," she said.

"And your mother is still friends with his mother?"

"Best friends," she added.

I would later learn how Jennifer's mother put pressure on her to drop the charges, failing to provide her with the critical support she needed.

In 2001, Thomas was arrested three times for assaulting Jennifer. All his cases were before Judge Arlene Ford, the misdemeanor domestic violence judge.

"I'm issuing an order of protection. You are to stay away from Jennifer Fine," the Judge warned.

"I don't want an order," Jennifer screamed from a bench in the courtroom. Her eyes were glassy; I think she was high.

Thomas was always trying to manipulate his way out of trouble. By coming to court with Jennifer, Thomas was trying to convey to the judge that everything was alright between them. But the judge wasn't buying it.

"I don't care what you want. This has been going on for too long. This is my order and I am issuing a full order of protection. If you violate this order one more time I am putting you in jail," the judge yelled at Thomas.

But the judge's warning fell on deaf ears. A few months later, Thomas was arrested again and Judge Ford kept her word, sending him to jail for two months. Thomas ended up pleading guilty on his cases and a full order of protection was issued for Jennifer.

I heard from Jennifer a year later, after Thomas punched her in the head for not spending Valentine's Day with him. Once again Thomas was released on low bail and a full order of protection was issued, prohibiting him from going to Jennifer's home. "That's my home too," Thomas declared. The court had no choice but to order a hearing since Thomas was claiming that the state was violating his constitutional rights by excluding him from his home. The standard was simple: If the court found that there was an imminent threat of harm to Jennifer, then the court could exclude Thomas, regardless of whether he lived there or not.

Unfortunately, Judge Ford was no longer sitting in Criminal Court. That meant that another judge would hold the hearing. Judge Sylvester, who had a reputation for giving the prosecution a difficult time, would now be in charge.

"Jennifer, Thomas is claiming that he lives with you in the apartment," I said when I called her on the phone.

"He hasn't paid a dime towards rent or bills. He lives with his mother, not with me."

"Well, we have to prove that to a judge, so I need you to come to my office next week to testify at a hearing," I said.

"Alright, I'll be there," she promised.

But she never came. Nor did she show up on the next three dates. So on the fourth date, I sent detectives to her home at 7:00 a.m. to personally escort her to the courthouse.

Judge Sylvester called us up to the bench to conference the case. That's when the defense attorney went off, telling the judge how Thomas was being framed by a jealous woman. Judge Sylvester was actually entertaining this blame–the–victim tirade, nodding her head up and down with a look of interest. "Your honor, the only issue before this court is whether Thomas poses an imminent threat of harm to Ms. Fine," I said, reminding the judge as to why we were there.

"Ms. Kaminsky, I know what the standard is and I don't need you to remind me," snapped the judge.

Jennifer nervously walked towards the witness stand, crying throughout the proceeding. It wasn't just the pain and humiliation of reliving the events but the treatment of the court, the way the judge continuously scolded her while Thomas sat in his seat with a big smirk on his face.

Jennifer tended to expound on her answers to my questions, which infuriated the judge. At one point, the judge got so angry that she told me to take Jennifer outside and explain to her how she should conduct herself in a court of law.

When we came back inside, the judge reminded Jennifer to only respond to the questions asked. Jennifer apologized, letting the judge know that she was very upset by the whole proceeding. Instead of showing a modicum of compassion, the judge snapped at Jennifer for interrupting her.

Throughout my questioning, the defense attorney was jumping up and down objecting like a jack in the box, trying to confuse Jennifer, and interrupt my train of thought. Instead of putting an end to the defense attorney's behavior, and creating a less intimidating environment for Jennifer, Judge Sylvester warned me that she would hold me in contempt if I didn't respect her rulings.

Hold me in contempt! I could barely contain my contempt.

It took three hours to complete the hearing. Jennifer was a compelling witness so Judge Sylvester had no choice but to issue a full order of protection barring Thomas from the home. But that didn't end the matter. Unless Thomas pleaded guilty to the underlying assault charge, I would have to prove his guilt at a trial, and that meant that Jennifer would have to testify again.

A month later, Jennifer left me a voicemail message stating that she didn't want the order of protection anymore. I tried calling her back but her number had been disconnected. I then wrote her a letter explaining that in light of the history of abuse, I would not change the order unless she came to my office and explained her reasons in person. But Jennifer never responded to me.

On the next court date, the defense attorney requested that the order of protection be changed to a limited order allowing contact between them. I explained to the judge that while Jennifer had indeed left me a voicemail message, I was unwilling to request a limited order until I had spoken with her in person since I had no idea what the circumstances were for her change of mind and whether Thomas was pressuring her to do so. Judge Sylvester called us up to the bench so there would be no record of our discussions. The judge told me that the state had no power to interfere in people's relationships and that she was not going to "infantilize" Ms. Fine. Thomas was smirking as the judge issued a limited order of protection.

When I tried to make a record as to the grounds for my objection, the judge cut me off, telling me, "the record that is made is the record that I say."

I couldn't believe it. Was this the same judge who found Thomas to be a danger to Jennifer just one month prior? Judge Sylvester, whether consciously or unconsciously, was colluding with the defendant, allowing him access to the very woman he had been abusing.

As I was about to leave the courtroom, my beeper went off. It was the assigned social worker. Jennifer was on her other line calling from Connecticut. She had gone there to get away from Thomas. Jennifer wanted to know why Thomas wasn't in jail, since she had an open police report against him. When I walked back into the courtroom to tell the judge, Thomas ran out the door. He must have known from the look on my face.

Two months later, Thomas was arrested. "Who's handling my case?" Thomas asked the detective.

"ADA Kaminsky," he replied.

"That bitch hates me," Thomas responded.

REFLECTIONS OF A DOMESTIC VIOLENCE PROSECUTOR

This time Thomas was charged with a felony. Jennifer was subpoenaed to appear in court. That morning she left me a voicemail message stating that she was too frightened to cooperate. It would be another three months before I would hear from her.

At the end of October 2002, Jennifer called me. She was frantic. Thomas had been leaving threatening messages on her voice mail. Jennifer said that she wanted him arrested and that she was ready to pursue criminal charges. That's the night Jennifer came to my office with her little girl.

But within a month, Jennifer was no longer returning my calls. Finding Jennifer was a formidable, but not impossible task. She didn't leave a forwarding address after being evicted from her apartment, or a new telephone number after her old one was disconnected. The one person who always knew how to reach her was Thomas, so it was no surprise to learn that he had called her five times on Valentine's Day, the day I combed through his inmate phone records.

At the next court proceeding, Thomas' lawyer handed the judge a letter that was allegedly written by Jennifer. In it, Jennifer claimed that all the police complaints she filed against Thomas were made at a time when she was emotionally unstable and worried about money. She went on to claim that instead of taking responsibility for her financial situation, she blamed Thomas. She ended the letter by claiming that she was the real aggressor in the relationship but that she couldn't discuss it in detail on the ground that she might incriminate herself.

I knew that Thomas was behind that letter, and I was convinced that his lawyer helped Jennifer write it. It didn't matter that Thomas was beating Jennifer, at least not to his attorney. His paramount goal was to get his client off the hook. The truth, in that process, was irrelevant.

I had to remember that I was seeking justice within an imperfect system, with prosecutors warring against judges who just don't get it, and defense attorneys who just don't care; where batterers are able to exploit a crime victim's financial, emotional and family issues to their advantage. In that system, men like Thomas are often the victors, while women like Jennifer, the casualties.

I had to remember that I was seeking justice within an imperfect system...

But it doesn't have to be this way. There are ways to rectify these imperfections. With stronger laws we can institute a paradigm shift that requires the law to hold offenders' accountable, not their victims.

Batterers like Thomas Cross need to be held accountable the moment they enter the criminal justice system. Accountability requires judges to view their criminal acts in their appropriate context, rather than as isolated incidents.[188] For example, the Valentine's Day assault on Jennifer was not an isolated incident, but part of a pattern of coercive behavior directed at Jennifer.[189] When dealing with batterers, judges must look at the prior history of abuse to understand the real nature of the batterers conduct, and use that information in determining whether bail should be set.

In this case, the arraignment judge was only considering the one act before the court, a minor misdemeanor assault, carrying minimal jail time. And the judge was only allowed to consider whether Thomas was a flight risk, not whether he was a threat to Jennifer's safety.[190]

Now imagine how this case could have turned out if there was a statutory bail scheme that allowed the arraignment judge to consider all of Thomas' behavior toward Jennifer, impose bail conditions like monitoring through global positioning system (GPS) devices, or order preventive detention if the judge felt that no conditions of release could assure Jennifer's safety.

While historically bail was a way to ensure a defendants return to court,[191] in 1984, the Federal Bail Reform Act expanded the scope and purpose of bail to include danger assessments.[192] The Act allows federal judges to impose bail conditions or order preventive detention if it's determined, after a hearing, that no conditions of bail can ensure the safety of a victim.[193] Many states have followed suit.[194] In fact, some states have responded to the danger posed by batterers by enacting specific bail statutes for domestic violence crimes.[195] Up until 2012, New York only allowed judges to consider whether a defendant was a flight risk when setting bail.[196]

If a risk assessment had been completed by law enforcement after the initial interview with Jennifer, and provided to the judge at the arraignment for the Valentine's Day assault, the judge would have been aware of Thomas' lengthy domestic violence history, and the real threat he posed to Jennifer.[197] Armed with that information and a meaningful bail statute, the judge could have either refused to set bail and issued a pre-trial detention order, or set high bail with the condition that if Thomas made bail, he would have to wear a GPS device.

And if Thomas were to violate any of his bail conditions, like the order of protection, the amended bail statute would require that in addition to forfeiting his bail, the sentence on each new violation would run consecutively to the original offense.[198] These sanctions might provide the meaningful deterrent that the law has thus far failed to provide.

After all, every time Thomas was arrested his mother bailed him out because the monetary amount was insignificant. If the bail was high, say at $25,000 cash or bond, Thomas' mother would either lose $25,000 cash, or lose the collateral she would have to give the bail bondsman to qualify for a bond. Thomas's mother owned the house where he lived. If the house was the collateral being put up, and Thomas was informed that his mother's home would be lost if he violated the order of protection, I wonder whether he would have continued to violate the order.

Likewise, I wonder whether Thomas would have continued to violate the order of protection if he were being monitored by a GPS device. And if he did violate the order of protection while the GPS device was in place, imagine how the court proceedings would have looked if the evidence came from uncontroverted data recorded in the GPS device, rather than Jennifer. Imagine what that would have meant to Jennifer if the District Attorney's Office didn't have to rely on her to hold Thomas accountable.

Also, imagine how different this case could have been if the judge presiding over it was sensitive to the complex issues arising out of domestic violence prosecutions, and the conflicting emotions of its victims.[199]

Finding such judges requires a meaningful screening process for judges are merely human, subject to the same troubling beliefs and behaviors as other mere mortals.[200] While domestic violence court parts

JUDGES & DEFENSE ATTORNEYS

have sprung up throughout the United States, specialized court parts are meaningless if the judges presiding over them lack the appropriate qualifications.[201]

Given the complexity of domestic violence prosecutions, judicial screening committees must select judges handling these cases, rather than leaving it to the sole discretion of administrative judges.[202] In addition to having representatives from the judiciary, defense bar, and district attorney's office, these newly formed screening committees should include academics and non-profit organizations that specialize in domestic violence.[203] These additional voices will ensure a more meaningful and thoughtful selection process. The committees must also continue to monitor their appointments. Confidential interviews of attorneys who appear before the judges, as well as victims who testified before the courts, should be conducted. Anonymity is critical so that people can speak openly about their experiences before the judge.

Finally, judges need to view criminal acts of batterers in the context of coercive control.[204] Judges must also be conscious of the way batterers use the criminal justice system to perpetuate their abuse.[205] Unlike stranger crimes, a batterer in the criminal justice system has access to his victim. Thomas was always able to find Jennifer, even when he was in jail, leaving him in a unique position to coerce her out of testifying against him.

In early 2000, when I was prosecuting Thomas, I didn't have access to his jail house phone conversations. Now these phone calls are provided to the District Attorney's Office routinely giving us the opportunity to show that batterers, by their pleas and promises are directly responsible for their victims not testifying.[206]

Implementing these reforms would send a powerful message to batterers. They would no longer be allowed to manipulate the system. And they would quickly see how committing acts of domestic violence will cause a forfeiture of their liberty and property. Maybe then there will be a reduction in domestic violence.

Mental Illness & Substance Abuse: *People v. Henry Edwards*

I HAD GONE TO the Criminal Court that day to speak with Denise's lawyer. I feel like I am entering the bowels of the world whenever I step through the doors of that old dirty limestone building at 120 Schermerhorn Street. It's the courthouse where Brooklyn's low level offenders are sent to answer for their crimes, and where nearly eight thousand domestic violence cases are handled each year. By 9:30 a.m., the line to get inside snakes around the corner onto Smith Street in downtown Brooklyn. Hundreds of defendants stand ready to empty their pockets, take off their belts and cell–phones, and place them into the stacks of plastic containers that travel through the X–ray scanners. No matter how much metal they unload, those machines always seem to go off. And when they do, the court officers are ready with their scanning wands, making sure they aren't armed, that it's safe to send them inside. This is a daily ritual in the Criminal Court.

The 9:30 commute on the elevator reminds me of rush hour on the subway. Everyone piles in, pushing into one another. Defendants, sporting oversized designer jeans, stand beside suited lawyers. Most of the men are young and black and wear outfits with names like "Sean John" and "Rocawear" prominently displayed on their jackets and shirts. They wear Du–rags and baseball caps on their heads and expensive name brand sneakers on their feet as they shout out lyrics to rap songs blaring from their head phones. One can always count on a little profanity to accompany the ride.

MENTAL ILLNESS & SUBSTANCE ABUSE

The courtrooms are gray and depressing. I'm always struck by the elegant courtrooms on Law & Order and the grim reality of ours. The defendants sit on benches that are carved with graffiti and plastered with the remnants of discarded gum.

The courtrooms are gray and depressing. I'm always struck by the elegant courtrooms on Law & Order and the grim reality of ours. The defendants sit on benches that are carved with graffiti and plastered with the remnants of discarded gum. Some doze off, while others strike up conversations, bonding together as they wait for their cases to be called.

My boss had called me into her office a few weeks prior, deeply troubled by Denise's case. It was my job to do the impossible: get Denise help. I remember leaving her office feeling like I had been asked to push a ten ton boulder up a hill.

Denise looked disheveled when she showed up in court for slicing her boyfriend's hand with a knife after he slapped her in the face. Denise had been in a slew of violent relationships. One particularly violent relationship cost her boyfriend his life. Denise was now involved with Henry Edwards, an unemployed career criminal with a penchant for malt liquor.

It was a busy day when Denise and Henry Edwards came before the judge. "I'm issuing orders of protection for each of you, stay away from each other or you will be arrested again," the judge warned before calling the next case. Two weeks later, Edwards was back again; this time, for punching Denise in the arm.

Five days later, Denise came to my office. Denise was short and heavy and wore a bandana around her head. She was nothing like my first impression of her in the Criminal Court building. She had a rough edge but she was also funny and thoughtful.

She'd had a tough life growing up in the projects surrounded by drug dealers, addicts and criminals. She was only thirty-two and already had six children by six different men. Denise was a loner with few friends. When she started to speak about her children, she softened. She told me how they had all been removed by the Administration for Children's Services and placed in foster care because she couldn't take care of them. She was an alcoholic with a psychiatric history, and a host of health related problems.

Denise told me how she had killed her boyfriend two years prior in the very apartment in which she was now living with Henry Edwards. The fight started over a game of dominoes that Denise was winning. "Fucking Ho," George screamed, angry that he was losing. He picked up his wooden stick, and beat her on the head, arms and legs. Denise grabbed a knife and stabbed him in the heart, killing him instantly. They had been dating for only eight months. Denise was cleared of all criminal charges after an investigation revealed that she had acted in self-defense.

I tried to speak to Denise about treatment for her alcoholism, about what it could do for her life, her children's lives, and her future. She politely listened, but refused to commit to anything, telling me she needed to think it over.

Then, a few weeks later Denise called me out of the blue, stating that she wanted to go away for treatment, get her life together and her children back, that she was "sick" of the way she was living and that she was "sick" of ending up with the same type of men.

On Denise's next court date, I met with her lawyer in the dimly lit hallway outside of the courtroom. Defendants were milling about, some with their girlfriends and children by their side.

I tried to negotiate a deal with Denise's lawyer, a former prosecutor who was now in private practice. He had been assigned by the court, and was being paid by the state for his services. This was my proposal: Denise would enter a long-term residential alcohol treatment center. If she successfully completed the program, then all criminal charges for assaulting Edwards would be dismissed. If she failed to complete the program, she would have to serve a jail sentence of six months.

MENTAL ILLNESS & SUBSTANCE ABUSE

Creating a plan for Denise took place within the limits of the criminal justice system, an adversarial system where the paramount goal of the defense is to get the client the best possible deal, not necessarily to find creative solutions for a client's life problems.

Creating a plan for Denise took place within the limits of the criminal justice system, an adversarial system where the paramount goal of the defense is to get the client the best possible deal, not necessarily to find creative solutions for a client's life problems. In keeping with that system, Denise's lawyer advocated for the least amount of jail time, insisting on three months rather than six if she failed to complete the program. But due to the sentencing laws, an inmate in the city correctional system only serves 2/3 of the sentence. That meant that Denise would only have to serve sixty days if she failed to complete the program, hardly an incentive to stay in an eighteen-month residential treatment program.

I was so frustrated at the lawyer's intransigence, at his inability to see the larger picture—that Denise was on a self-destructive path either to kill again or be killed. I told him that talking to him was like "talking to a wall." He accused me of insulting him and stormed off, ending our conversation.

Admitting defeat isn't easy, especially for me. The truth was that Henry Edwards refused to cooperate in Denise's criminal prosecution, and without his testimony I had no case. If I didn't agree to a plea, the case would be dismissed, and there would be no chance of helping Denise. That left me with no other choice but to agree to the defense attorney's conditions.

On her next court date, Denise pleaded guilty. I had this one moment to act, but a lack of resources stood in the way. There were no beds available in any of the treatment centers used by the court and funded by Medicaid, and being poor and without insurance, Denise couldn't afford a private facility. Denise had no choice but to return to the same neighborhood where she had been drinking for over twenty years.

A month later, Denise was admitted to the "G" building, the infamous psychiatric wing of Kings County Hospital. When she was finally released I couldn't understand her because her thoughts were jumbled. The one thing she was clear about was that she would not go away for treatment.

I still held on to a glimmer of hope that someone could convince Denise otherwise. That person was Denise's counselor, who had been working with her for years. I remember that phone call, the urgency in my voice. But the counselor was matter of fact, even cynical, telling me that she had been down this road with Denise many times before.

A couple of weeks later Denise was arrested for assaulting her next-door neighbor in the hallway of her apartment building. With treatment no longer an option, Denise was sentenced to serve three months in jail for the assault on Edwards and her neighbor.

In the meantime Edwards had been sitting in jail on his felony case, unable to come up with the bail money. Edwards was only thirty-nine and had already spent four years in prison for robbery. The judge eventually released him when I disclosed that I would be unable to try the case without Denise. Edwards was still required to report to court every few weeks, until his case was dismissed under New York State's speedy trial statute, under which I was required to try him within six months of his arrest. Edwards had a habit of expressing his disgust at this inconvenience by muttering under his breath, clicking his tongue and hissing.

The last time I saw him he was wearing sunglasses with one pant leg rolled up to his knee. He sat down on the bench and swung his leg over the armrest as he waited for his case to be called, like he was sitting on his own personal couch rather than on a bench in a court of law. When the judge told him that his case wouldn't be dismissed for another two weeks, he became rude, telling the judge how he wasted subway fare just to be there. I knew it would only be a matter of time before Edwards came back.

Three month later, he was arrested for armed robbery.

MENTAL ILLNESS & SUBSTANCE ABUSE

A holistic approach with a collaborative inter-disciplinary team is essential to effectively addressing the needs of battered women.

A year later, Denise died from a long term illness. At the time of her death, there were three criminal cases pending against Henry Edwards for assaulting her.

Looking back at this case, I realize how a multidisciplinary approach was critical. I was not only limited in my understanding of Denise's problems, but in my ability to resolve the profound social and economic issues she faced. Cases like these require a high risk domestic violence response team composed of various specialists working collaboratively.[207]

Many District Attorney's Offices have co-located services like Family Justice Centers, but not a collaborative team approach to their cases.[208] Yet, prosecutors are often the first to unearth the complex issues confronting victims of domestic violence. Our inability to adequately address one issue adversely affects our ability to address others, like safety planning.[209] A holistic approach with a collaborative inter-disciplinary team is essential to effectively addressing the needs of battered women.[210]

If I had worked in conjunction with a team of professionals consisting of mental health providers knowledgeable about the mental hygiene laws, a domestic violence advocate and domestic violence police officers, we could have sat down at the table and fashioned a treatment plan responsive to Denise's particular situation.[211]

How could I have expected Denise to agree to treatment when she was living in the very same environment where she had been drinking and drugging for over twenty years with no support system? If there was a high risk response team in place, we could have divided up home visits to her on a frequent basis using the resources of social service providers, domestic violence police officers, and representatives from the district attorney's office. We also could have worked with Denise to find her a meaningful support system through local non-profit organizations, religious institutions, AA meetings and the like.[212]

I believe that it could have made a difference, given that it did in the case of John Smith, a case I handled years prior. John was a mentally ill eighteen year-old who stabbed his father because he thought he was the devil. John's father refused to press charges because he wanted his son to get help, but did not want to involve the criminal justice system. While I explained to John's father that the criminal case would provide an incentive for John to stay in residential treatment, he couldn't bring himself to testify against his son. Given the serious nature of the charges, I pursued a case using evidence other than the testimony of John's dad. John remained in jail during the pendency of the case, housed on a mental health unit.

While in jail, and stabilized on anti-psychotic medication, John, with the support of his family, agreed to a plea offer of long term residential treatment. A few years later, I attended a conference on mental illness and the criminal justice system. John was one of their speakers. He spoke to the audience about the way his life had turned around, how he was now on medication living in an assisted living facility. He was happy; so were his parents. They too had found support through the treatment center, meeting regularly with other parents of mentally ill children, people who could identify with their experiences.

A confluence of events appears to have enabled John to accept treatment and turn his life around. For starters, John was immediately stabilized on medication; he had loving supportive parents who were actively involved in his treatment; and he continued to be supported and monitored by a mental health system even after his court case ended.

We need to replicate that model and give people like Denise those same support systems. Maybe then we can provide the meaningful change that women like Denise so desperately need.

4

Safety

RISK ASSESSMENTS (also known as danger, threat and lethality assessments) are used by numerous battered women's service providers to calculate a woman's risk of re-abuse based on the presence of certain factors.[213] These factors have been culled from studies of women who have either been killed or survived attacks by their intimate partners, and from men who have killed their intimate partners.[214] Such factors include recent separation, extreme jealousy, access to a gun, previous threats with a weapon, stalking, sexual abuse, abuse during pregnancy and substance abuse.[215]

In order to assess the dangerousness of a particular woman's situation, prosecutors and advocates in my office ask a series of questions about the history of abuse. Most of my career prosecuting domestic violence cases, I used this information merely to formulate legal arguments in court, rather than to address a woman's safety. I simply failed to see that my role extended beyond building a successful criminal prosecution. I also failed to appreciate how the answers shed light on the risks women faced of either being re-victimized or worse, murdered.

Because prosecutors are often battered women's first point of contact, it's imperative that we tell women the significance of the questions and their answers. One of our primary goals during an interview should be to educate women about their risk of being the victims of future violence, and how their level of danger is fluid, changing with their particular circumstances.[216] Since many women don't want to go forward with criminal prosecution, we must stress that regardless of their desire to proceed with the criminal case, they need to be vigilant and have a safety plan in place.

While these assessments are not foolproof,[217] they do provide women with critical information to help gauge their own safety, and they can be useful even for women who feel they can reliably predict their partners' level of violence towards them.[218] Every service provider that has contact with women who have been battered should administer these assessments so that they can engage women in a discussion about their level of danger.[219]

Prosecutors need to do this because we see first-hand how many women continue their relationships in spite of the abuse. Yet, we know that the majority of men who abuse don't change.[220] That means that women are in constant danger of re-abuse. While the risk of lethal violence is much rarer than re-abuse, we must inform women that while there is no way of knowing for certain who is capable of murder, they must be ever mindful of the danger they face from their partners.[221] Also, if a woman is planning on separating from her abuser, we need to inform her that studies have determined that separation is a very dangerous time.[222]

In addition to risk assessments, my office provides safety planning in the form of home alarms, 911-connected cell phones, shelter placement and housing relocation. Another tool that should be used with recidivist batterers and domestic violence parolees is 24/7 monitoring with global positioning system (GPS)devices.[223] This is the only way to ensure that the most dangerous offenders are under constant surveillance.

In a study of thirty-one men who killed their intimate partners, three of the killers, when asked about potential deterrents, claimed that technology in the form of real-time monitoring would most likely have deterred them from committing murder.[224] Two of these men had active restraining orders against them at the time of the murders, with both claiming that the orders were not a deterrent.[225]

The following cases illustrate the ever-present dangers confronting women, and how conversations regarding safety could have changed the course of their lives.

Separation & Jealousy
People v. Hector Sanchez

HECTOR SANCHEZ SAT at the defense table next to his lawyer with a sad, vacant look. It was hard to believe that such a little man was capable of so much violence, of beating and suffocating his forty–eight–year–old wife to death.

Liliana Alvarez represented the immigrant success story. She had fled Puerto Rico twenty years before with her three young children, leaving behind a physically abusive alcoholic husband. Her son told me how hard she worked to learn English, highlighting the words from her school book then looking them up in the dictionary. She worked during the day and put herself through school at night, eventually earning a college degree in social work. At the time of her death, she was the director of a social services agency in the Bronx. By all accounts she was a loving mother, hard worker, and supportive friend.

In 1987, she met Hector Sanchez in the hallway of her building. Hector had just come over from Bolivia and was staying with his brother, who lived in the same apartment building. Five years later they married.

After her death, her friends told me about the black eyes and bruises to her face. Liliana never admitted that it was Hector. "I fell down the stairs," she would say. But they all suspected otherwise.

In 1996, Liliana and Hector bought a two–family home. Liliana provided the down payment and paid the bills while Hector squandered his money on liquor. That was a constant source of fighting. Things got worse when Hector brought his teenage daughter, Bianca, over from

Bolivia. Hector was never home, so the responsibility for taking care of Bianca fell on Liliana. Liliana was the one who had to discipline her when she cut school or failed to do her homework. This caused more tension in the house. By 1999, Liliana asked Hector to leave.

I met Bianca a few months before the trial. She was living with her mother in a small working class town just outside New York City. A bunch of children's toys was scattered on the front lawn when I pulled into the driveway. Bianca's mother, Josephine, met me at the door. There was a pendant hanging from her neck with a picture of her three children: Bianca, her little boy and baby girl. We sat down in the living room and spoke about her relationship with Hector in Bolivia sixteen years earlier. She cried throughout our conversation.

Josephine told me how she met Hector at fifteen when she was attending an all girls Catholic high school. She passed by the construction site where he worked every morning on her way to school. He was the first man who ever paid attention to her. Hector was six years older.

A few months later she was pregnant. Her father was a strict Catholic and insisted that they marry. Josephine moved in with Hector and his mother. Hector soon became violent. He would beat and rape her when he drank. Josephine eventually moved back home with her father.

Then one day Hector came and took Bianca. Josephine was too young to fight Hector and his mother for custody. Tears were streaming down her face as she told me how she waited each day on a street corner just to get a glimpse at Bianca. Josephine eventually left Bolivia and came to New York. She told me how she now felt complete, as she smiled lovingly at Bianca, who was busy playing with her half brother and sister.

Bianca then shared with me about her brief stay with Hector and Liliana. She told me how sometimes she would awaken in the middle of the night and find her father standing at the foot of her bed staring at her. Liliana's adult daughter recounted the very same disturbing behavior.

Hector started stalking Liliana soon after she told him to leave. In the morning he'd show up at her bus stop, and in the evening he'd hang out across the street from her job. She was so unnerved by his behavior that she applied for an order of protection from the Family Court, prohibiting him from having any contact with her.

SEPARATION & JEALOUSY

Countless batterers threaten to kill their victims each and every day in Brooklyn. Only a crystal ball could have revealed that Hector would be the one to make good on that threat a year and a half later.

In February of 1999, while that order was in effect, Hector called Liliana on the telephone. "Are you seeing another man? If you are I will shoot you. Maybe not today or tomorrow but I will shoot you," he assured her. Liliana filed a report with the local police precinct and Hector was arrested for violating the order of protection. A few days later Liliana came to the District Attorney's Office. But she didn't want Hector prosecuted because she didn't believe that Hector would ever act on that threat. She was also not ready to cut all ties. Liliana was the only witness to the threatening call, and without her testimony, the charges could not be proven. As a result, the case was eventually dismissed.

Countless batterers threaten to kill their victims each and every day in Brooklyn.[226] Only a crystal ball could have revealed that Hector would be the one to make good on that threat a year and a half later.

Hector and Liliana continued to see each other. Liliana also started dating Leo Perez, a man from her neighborhood. On September 1, 2000, Liliana went out for drinks with Hector and her closest friend, Jorge Ramon. At approximately 1:00 a.m. Liliana and Hector headed back to his single room occupancy on Knickerbocker Avenue in Bushwick. On the way, they stopped at a store to buy some beer. Hector reached inside Liliana's pocketbook to get some cash and found a picture of Liliana and Leo. They argued all the way back to his place.

There were four rooms in the basement of the building where Hector lived. The tenants used sheets as makeshift doors. With so little privacy, it was impossible for the other occupants on the floor not to have heard

Liliana's cries that night. Yet no one did anything to help her as she was being murdered.

The Brooklyn North Coalition, a grass roots domestic violence advocacy group, held a candlelight march one month after Liliana's murder. We walked from the 83rd Precinct all the way up Knickerbocker Avenue to the building where Liliana was killed. The leader of the coalition stood out front with a bullhorn shaming the tenants inside for failing to call 911. One call may have saved her life.

Wanted posters with Hector's face were taped on poles throughout Bushwick. A month later the police received a tip from an anonymous call to 911. Hector was inside a bodega a few blocks from the precinct. He had disguised himself with a baseball cap, eyeglasses and a full beard.

I spoke with Hector at the precinct the night he was arrested. Hector remembered everything he did the day of the murder: how he went to work, how he went over to Jorge's home, how they all went out to dinner, how they ate and how he took Liliana back to his place. Hector remembered going into Liliana's bag to get some singles and finding a picture of Liliana and Leo. He remembered that he was angry and that he was fighting with her. He also remembered entering his building and walking down the stairs with her. He remembered losing control when he was in the room. But as to the actual events in the room that night, Hector had a convenient bout of amnesia.

The pictures of Liliana's naked body on the autopsy table were taped to a large piece of oak–tag that hung behind the witness stand in the courtroom. I told her children about the graphic photos, but they insisted on staying in the courtroom. They sat there stoically as the medical examiner testified in clinical terms about the autopsy: the bruises to Liliana's face, arms, legs, and stomach, the fractured rib, the lacerated tongue, the semen in her anus, the semen in her vagina.

At trial, a defense psychiatrist would offer a medical explanation for Hector's amnesia. After two brief interviews with Hector, Dr. Simons, the defense expert, concluded that Hector suffered from brain damage due to twenty–five years of alcohol abuse, and that such damage significantly impaired his attention, memory and concentration. It was this alleged damage that allegedly prevented Hector from forming the necessary mental state to commit murder.

SEPARATION & JEALOUSY

Dr. Simons simply ignored the fact that Hector was a highly functioning individual up until the day of the murder. He was a short–order cook and deliveryman who was responsible for preparing a variety of dishes and then delivering them in his car. His boss testified that he was an excellent worker who had no problems following orders, reading recipes or driving.

The jury saw right through the expert and came back with a murder conviction after a few short hours of deliberations.

Liliana's son, David, spoke at the sentencing. The law allows family members to make such statements.[227] It might give you "closure," I tell them, "to confront the perpetrator face to face." As if a five minute statement can ever close the wound of the murder of a loved one.

David spoke about the impact his mother's death had on his family. He came into the well of the courtroom and stood next to me, with his thoughts written neatly on a piece of paper. Softly he spoke, turning occasionally to look at Hector, who sat just a few feet away. It was heart–wrenching listening to David speak about the images indelibly etched in his mind of his mother's last few minutes of life, "dying alone, scared, brutalized by a man that she once loved."

Hector Sanchez sat there staring down at the table, the same way he did throughout the trial. The judge then sentenced him to twenty–four years to life, taking one year off the maximum sentence because he had never been in trouble with the law.

This was a straightforward case. The murder was the culmination of a physically abusive relationship, where the abuser finally lost control of his victim.[228]

I am left wondering whether our brief interaction with Liliana could have been more productive. What if we had engaged her in a meaningful discussion about the risks to her safety given that certain risk factors, namely recent separation, jealousy, stalking, and alcoholism, were present in her relationship?[229] If these risk factors had been explained to Liliana, and she were told to keep them in the forefront of her mind, she might have taken more precautions in her interactions with Hector. For example, she may not have carried around a picture of Leo Perez, the other man she was seeing, and she might not have gone alone to Hector's basement apartment. She might have confined her meetings with Hector to places where others were present, like her own home where her children resided.

Prosecutors must educate and inform women at the first available opportunity. I don't mean talking at women, but engaging them in a meaningful conversation about their safety. It means acknowledging the reality—the elephant in the room that we never discuss in our interviews—that most women will go back to their abusers. With that understanding, prosecutors must tell women that their safety is our primary concern, regardless of their desire to proceed with the prosecution or return to their abusers.

We need to do this so we can build trust with women, and hope they will share with us information critical to formulating an effective safety plan.[230] If we judge them or criticize their choices, we can be sure they won't share with us information that just may help save their lives.[231]

Children & Financial Dependence
People v. Carlos Montero

MEN LIKE CARLOS always have a woman by their side. They have a way of charming them, gaining their trust and love.[232] This romantic phase is usually short-lived and disappears by the time they get them pregnant. But by then it's too late. Now they are tied together by children, making escape all the more difficult. That's what happened to Lourdes.

Lourdes was seventeen when she met Carlos in her small town just outside of Santo Domingo. Carlos was nearly twenty years her senior and already had four children with three different women. Carlos was short, stocky and bald. Lourdes was tall, slim and pretty, with long brown hair and dark chocolate eyes.

Carlos left the Dominican Republic for New York while Lourdes was pregnant with Christina. Once he settled in, he brought them over. They moved in with Carlos's sister and husband in Washington Heights, a largely Dominican community. I met Pedro and Luisa in my office in 2002, two years after Lourdes's murder. They sat in the chair across from my desk with an interpreter by their side. First Luisa, then Pedro. They both responded defensively when I asked them what they did when Carlos beat Lourdes. "That was their business," they each said.

In October of 1996, after being in the country for less than a year, Lourdes got a job with her cousin Tania at a restaurant in the Bronx. Carlos had a habit of calling Lourdes a whore, accusing her of cheating on

REFLECTIONS OF A DOMESTIC VIOLENCE PROSECUTOR

...prosecutors must tell women that their safety is our primary concern, regardless of their desire to proceed with the prosecution or return to their abusers.

him with the men at the restaurant.[233] In late October of 1996, Lourdes was in the bedroom with her daughter, getting ready for work.

"Where do you think you're going?" Carlos said.

"I'm going to work," she replied.

"No you're not," he said before punching and kicking her. The beating lasted for six hours.

Christina, who was only two, ran to her mother. That's when Carlos whipped out the belt and smacked her across her tiny buttocks. Carlos then ripped off Lourdes's clothes, threw her on the bed, and continued to hit her in the face while he raped her. Lourdes would conceive a little boy as a result. When he was finished, he tore up the rest of her clothing. On the following day, after Carlos left, Lourdes took Christina to Tania's apartment in Brooklyn.

Two days later, while Lourdes was at work, she got a call from another cousin in Brooklyn, informing her that Carlos had taken Christina. Lourdes, Tania and Tania's boyfriend Enrique left the restaurant and drove to Washington Heights. Lourdes ran upstairs to the apartment to get her daughter as Tania and Enrique waited in the car. When Lourdes didn't come back, Tania called the police and then headed up to the apartment with Enrique.

Carlos pulled a knife on Enrique and threatened to stab him if he tried to take Lourdes and Christina. The police walked up the stairs just as Carlos was wielding the knife. That night Carlos was arrested.

From the start, law enforcement took this case seriously. The Manhattan District Attorney's Office prosecuted him for the most serious charges and refused to accept a plea deal of less than two and one-half to five years' imprisonment. The court issued an eight-year full order of protection and the division of parole refused him early release. Yet no one was able to prevent Lourdes from writing Carlos and giving him her new address. Nor was anyone watching Carlos twenty-four hours a day when he was released from prison, or guarding Lourdes's door the night he came to her apartment under the pretext of giving her money for the kids.

Carlos kept in touch with Lourdes while he was in prison, writing her letters and calling her on the phone, professing his love for her and their children. It was his way of winning her trust, letting her know that she had nothing to fear once he was released.

In the meantime Carlos was telling his fellow inmates at Watertown Correctional Facility in upstate New York how he was going to kill Lourdes when he was released, blaming her for taking four years of his life.[234] There was one inmate in particular that he confided in. That inmate was Ricardo Sanchez.

In June of 2000, Ricardo was reading the Daily News as he waited to see his parole officer. When he turned the page, he saw Carlos's picture with an article about Lourdes's murder. Ricardo immediately contacted the police.

The events in the courtroom can take on a surreal quality. That's how it was when Ricardo testified. Ricardo was a career criminal with a penchant for history and Hitchcock movies. He testified that as he was lying in his cell reading a biography of Harry Truman by David McCullough, Carlos proposed that they each kill the other's girlfriend.

"What did you say to him when he said that?" I asked.

"I asked him if he saw 'Strangers on the Train', an old Hitchcock movie starring Robert Walker and Bob Cummings, because it was the same thing where one guy would kill the other's wife," Ricardo responded with the utmost seriousness.

Christina came to court wearing her thick long brown hair slicked back in a tight bun. She wore a matching pink and black checked skirt and blazer with black Mary Janes on her feet. She looked just like her mother. Christina remembered it all. She remembered how her father came to their apartment and had a beer with her mother, how her mother took a pill because she had a headache, how her mother told her and her little brother to go to bed, how she woke up because her mother

REFLECTIONS OF A DOMESTIC VIOLENCE PROSECUTOR

All that horror permanently etched in the mind of a twelve-year-old child. No prison sentence could ever do justice for that.

was screaming, how she got out of bed and saw her father punching her mother and tying a string around her neck, how her mother yelled at her to call 911, how she picked up the phone but didn't know which numbers were 9–1–1, how Carlos grabbed the phone from her and smacked her across the face, how her mother fell to the ground and lay there motionless with her eyes open, how her father packed her clothes and her brother's clothes and took some CDs from the apartment, how her father sold the CDs to the cab driver as they drove to his sister's house in Washington Heights, how her aunt refused to keep them, how her father brought her back to Brooklyn and left her and her brother outside a cousin's building at 3:00 a.m., and how her father gave her ten dollars to keep quiet. All that horror permanently etched in the mind of a twelve-year-old child. No prison sentence could ever do justice for that.

Christina's pictures still hang on the walls across from my desk. A smiley face and colorful tulip made with glitter glue adorn one wall, the Power Puff Girl on the other. Everyone thinks that picture captures her sadness. "No," I tell them, "It's a Power Puff Girl." "See," I say as I point to the sad-shaped eyes of the Power Puff pin that hangs on my bulletin board with the caption "I'm having a moment." Christina was seven when she drew them, almost a year after she watched her father murder her mother. "My mommy was laying there with her eyes open," Christina told me as she sat in the chair across from my desk, her feet barely touching the floor.

After the murder there was a manhunt for Carlos. His photo appeared in the local papers and on the local news. The police scoured Kennedy Airport and the Port Authority. Airline security claimed to have seen a man fitting his description boarding a plane to Puerto Rico.

Others claimed that he was hiding out at a Christian compound in the Dominican Republic. A lone police officer on routine patrol in Florida would find him.

In August of 2002, Police Officer Felicia Santana of the Hialeah force observed a man make an illegal left hand turn at a busy intersection. Out came the sirens and lights. A few feet later, in the parking lot of a strip mall, she pulled the man over. Officer Santana approached the car and asked for his license and registration. The man said he didn't have any and gave the name of Juan Arias and a date of birth. Officer Santana went back to her car only to learn that no one by that name and date of birth had a driver's license in the state of Florida. When she went back to the car, she told him that he would be placed under arrest for driving without a license. He calmly complied with Officer Santana's directives.

"Place both hands on the hood of the car," she said.

"Spread your legs."

"Give me your left hand."

Just as Officer Santana was placing the handcuff on his left wrist the man jammed her in the face with his right elbow, spun her around and grabbed her from behind. Then came the blows to her face and body. Using all her body weight she managed to push him to the ground. That's when two males who were shopping in the mall jumped in and sat on top of him until other police units arrived. The man was Carlos. Two months later he was extradited to New York.

It was a chilly afternoon in early November when detectives brought him back from Florida. Lourdes's family was lined up against the wall glaring at Carlos as he came down the hallway of the courthouse, handcuffed and wearing an Hawaiian shirt and shorts. He never looked their way.

The evidence against Carlos was overwhelming. His little girl witnessed the crime, his fingerprints were on a beer bottle in the kitchen, and his DNA was underneath Lourdes's fingernails from her desperate attempts to claw away from him. Carlos needed some excuse for the murder so he hired a psychiatrist, someone who would claim that Carlos acted under an extreme emotional disturbance when he beat and strangled Lourdes. If the jury believed him, it would be a mitigating factor knocking the charge of murder down to manslaughter.

REFLECTIONS OF A DOMESTIC VIOLENCE PROSECUTOR

Safety planning is critical, for orders of protection are merely pieces of paper. They can't stop someone who is intent on harming.

Carlos took the witness stand, testifying without emotion. According to Carlos, he went to see Lourdes on that fateful June night in 2000 to give her money for the children. That's when she told him that he was not the father of her son. The shock of her words caused him to lose control. He reached for the nearest thing he could find, which was a shoelace, and tied it around her neck, pulling it until she fell to the floor. His story defied common sense, that Lourdes, who had already been the victim of his rage, would say such a thing when she was alone with him.

That's why Carlos hired Dr. Shyler, a forensic psychiatrist with an Ivy League education, someone who could add legitimacy to his claim. When I asked Dr. Shyler if it made sense that Lourdes would risk Carlos's wrath by telling him such a thing when she knew from first-hand experience what he was capable of doing to her, Dr. Shyler responded like this: "It's been my experience that sometimes women tragically fancy that by taunting a man they will have more satisfying sex." There was no need to ask him anything further. The jurors were disgusted, shaking their heads in disbelief.

Two hours after being charged, the jury returned a unanimous verdict of Murder in the Second Degree. Ten days later, Carlos was sentenced. Tania made a statement to the court, letting the judge know the impact Lourdes's murder had on their family, and the devastating consequences to Christina, who had to live with the memories for the rest of her life.

Carlos sat there without emotion staring straight ahead with that same icy glare.

The court then imposed a sentence of twenty-five years to life.

"Why don't you give me fifteen more," Carlos yelled at the judge.

He then turned to me and started screaming in Spanish, the spit flying from his mouth. The court interpreter translated his every word.

"You bitch, you daughter of a bitch."

Carlos was a killer without empathy or remorse.[235] He took no responsibility for assaulting and raping Lourdes. Instead, he blamed her for taking four years of his life. That is how batterers think; they have zero insight, believing everyone else is to blame but themselves.[236] This is why victims of domestic violence should never be lulled into a false sense of security just because law enforcement has entered their lives. Safety planning is critical, for orders of protection are merely pieces of paper. They can't stop someone who is intent on harming.[237]

This case also illustrates how safety is fluid.[238] Lourdes was safe for the four years Carlos was incarcerated. But as soon as he was released from prison he posed the same danger as before. While parole was responsible for monitoring him, they never did a safety plan with Lourdes to determine the scope and conditions of his monitoring. His parole was thus disconnected from the very crime that landed him there.

The criminal justice system needs to account for a victim's social and economic realities and their specific vulnerabilities at each stage of the process. A sufficient safety plan needed to account for the fact that Carlos was a violent felony offender who was being released to the same city where his victim and children lived.

Lourdes was an undocumented immigrant mother barely making ends meet. A meaningful discussion would have acknowledged her economic vulnerability and how Carlos could use it to his advantage to gain access to her.

Lourdes needed to be warned that she could never let her guard down with Carlos. There needed to be a discussion about different precautions to take, like never meeting him alone or in private.

Moreover, monitoring for someone like Carlos should have included a global positioning system (GPS) with real time monitoring.[239] If this was in place, the police would have been immediately notified when Carlos got within a certain range of Lourdes's home.[240]

Instead, Lourdes was all alone with two small children when Carlos was released back into the community with no one watching. It was a disaster waiting to happen.

5

A Successful Prosecution

A SUCCESSFUL PROSECUTION HAS two components: victim satisfaction and offender accountability. As a result of legislative, judicial and social reforms over the past thirty years, prosecutors have been able to achieve some level of success. While success has been less than complete due to the adversarial nature of the system, mandatory arrest laws, pro–prosecution policies, victim advocates, and domestic violence judges have helped ensure that every effort will be made to hold offenders accountable.

I have worked with many women who have benefited from these changes. They have seen their batterers arrested and brought before domestic violence judges who refused to minimize their batterers' actions. They have seen the resources of the district attorney's office, from subpoena power to the hiring of expert witnesses, used to enhance the prosecution of their cases. They have been in court when juries held their batterers accountable and judges imposed sentences commensurate with their crimes. For individual crime victims these things they have observed have tremendous meaning. So while the criminal justice system can't bring about systemic change for battered women, or consistently hold batterers accountable, each successful prosecution enables us to bring justice into the lives of individual women.

Battered women have also benefited from the creation of Family Justice Centers, in which a number of services are available in one location.[241] In 2005, the Brooklyn District Attorney's Office became the lead

A SUCCESSFUL PROSECUTION

Battered women have also benefited from the creation of Family Justice Centers, in which a number of services are available in one location.

partner in the creation of the Brooklyn Family Justice Center.[242] Housed on the same floor as the Domestic Violence Unit of the Brooklyn District Attorney's Office, the Family Justice Center has 23 partner agencies all in one location. Victims of domestic violence, whether or not pursuing criminal charges, can obtain help with housing and receive civil legal representation for divorce, custody, visitation, financial support, and immigration matters. The center also provides faith–based counseling, as well as therapeutic counseling for victims and their children. Although the economic picture for many victims is bleak with the minimum wage far below a living wage, a self–sufficiency coordinator provides a wide range of services, including referrals for job training and placement, access to public benefits, and educational opportunities like GED and English as a second language programs.[243] Partner agencies include non profit organizations that work with the Arabic, Asian, Orthodox Jewish, and Caribbean communities, with support services provided in many native languages. The Brooklyn District Attorney, Charles Hynes, actively encourages victims to use these services regardless of whether they choose to involve the criminal justice system.[244]

Thirty–five years ago, Del Martin, in her book, *Battered Wives*, documented a Florida domestic violence advocate's wish for co–located services.[245] It took close to thirty years to make this a reality. While funding is always in short supply, and more women need services than are currently available, battered women today have access to more services than they ever had in the history of the battered women's movement.

Achieving Justice
People v. Frank Brown

THE FRANK BROWN CASE epitomized the successful use of the criminal justice system to help empower a victim of domestic violence: how a woman finally received justice after being brutally beaten and sexually assaulted by her ex–boyfriend and then re–victimized by an emergency room doctor who ignored her claim of rape when he learned her ex–boyfriend was the perpetrator.

Rebecca Smith was a beautiful woman in her late forties who worked for a non–profit organization that helped troubled youth. She was also a gifted piano player. She was a prosecutor's dream witness, fitting society's historic definition of the deserving victim.[246]

In the late 1990s, her husband died after a protracted illness. A few years later, Rebecca met Frank at a neighborhood coffee shop. They became fast friends. Frank was kind and supportive during a difficult period in her life. They started dating a short time later.

Frank was thirteen years her junior and had a sporadic work history. When he had nowhere to stay, Rebecca let him live with her, a decision she would later regret. Frank stayed away for days at a time, hanging out at the club where he was a bouncer. Rebecca would come to learn about his drug problem, how he never had money to contribute for the rent, how she had to supplement his income because he was blowing his right up his nose. She would also learn about the mother of his child who had fled the state to escape his abuse.

She was a prosecutor's dream witness, fitting society's historic definition of the deserving victim.

After a few months, Rebecca stopped sleeping in bed with Frank, preferring to sleep on the living room couch. One day Rebecca had enough and wanted Frank out. He had been gone for weeks so she started locking the door with the dead bolt. It was five in the morning when she awoke to hear Frank banging and screaming at the front door. Rebecca called the police. The police told her that she couldn't just put him out since he had been living in her apartment for over thirty days.[247] Frank now had legal rights to Rebecca's apartment.

Rebecca went to the Housing Court and spoke with a lawyer who explained the process. He gave her a sample eviction notice that she could use as a template. Rebecca put the paper away in her closet, never suspecting that Frank was going through her papers when she wasn't home.

Rebecca had been out to dinner with a friend that fateful night. When she came into her apartment, Frank was waving the paper in his hand, screaming at her. Frank threw her on the sofa. "Why are you doing this to me, bitch?" he yelled with his hands around her neck. When he let go, he told her to get on the floor. When she wouldn't, he threw her down. Rebecca rolled herself up in a ball trying to protect herself from his repeated blows to the back of her neck and head.

"I have to go to the bathroom," she pleaded.

"You're not going anywhere," he said, as he reached for a bucket in the kitchen. That's where she was forced to urinate.

Frank pulled her dress off, and made her stay on the floor as he drank from a bottle of scotch. He then got on the ground, raping her vaginally and then sodomizing her as she screamed out in pain. When he was finished, he got up and went to the bedroom, returning with a pair of stockings. After he made her put them on, he cut the crotch with a knife, and then inserted his penis in her vagina, followed by the knife handle. He forced her to drink some water and then put his mouth on her vagina and told her to pee in his face.

Rebecca was pleading with him to stop. "Shut up, bitch," he yelled, as he drank from the bottle of scotch. The torture lasted for hours, with Frank taking breaks to watch sexually charged videos and snort cocaine.

Frank eventually dragged Rebecca into the bedroom, where he again raped her. When he finished, he passed out on the bed. Rebecca quietly walked out and tied the bedroom door to the hallway closet door with the phone cord, locking Frank inside. Rebecca then called 911 and ran to a neighbor's apartment. Rebecca's eye was swollen shut; five of her caps were knocked out of her mouth. Frank was lying naked on the bed when the police arrived.

It was a busy day for domestic violence arrests at the local precinct. The one domestic violence officer on duty was tending to Rebecca as well as other cases. In the frenzy of the day, the police officer forgot to charge Frank with Rape.

The defense attorney tried to use that omission to her advantage, vigorously cross-examining the officer at trial in an attempt to prove that Rebecca's claim of Rape was a lie. But the officer was honorable and fell on the sword, admitting that he, and not Rebecca, was to blame for his mistake.

Frank was writing letters and leaving messages on Rebecca's machine after he was arrested, begging her to drop the charges, asking her to think about what she was doing to his life. Apparently, what he had done to Rebecca was beside the point.

Rebecca sat on the witness stand and told the jury all the horrific details of what Frank had done to her that night. She was soft spoken and articulate. The jury listened intently. Then the defense attorney got up and began her cross-examination. Her tactic was to convince the jury that Rebecca was lying because Frank refused to marry her.

During the lunch break, the judge asked the defense attorney how long her questioning would last. He didn't want Rebecca on the stand any longer than was necessary. He believed her, and wanted it to end; so did the jury.

After a few hours of deliberation, the jury convicted Frank of multiple counts of Rape and Sodomy. Ten days later Frank was sentenced. Frank

Lin's husband started beating her on a regular basis. Whenever she would threaten to call the police, he would scream, "I am the law."

stood before the judge with his lawyer by his side and insisted that he had done nothing wrong that night. The judge then handed down a sentence commensurate with the crime, fifteen years' imprisonment, a sentence reserved for the most serious offenders.[248]

A year later, Rebecca invited me to one of her performances, which was held in a church in Manhattan. I sat in a pew watching Rebecca play the piano with such conviction. It was a profound experience for me, knowing that she almost lost her life the previous year and now was performing in the sanctity of the church. As I watched her, I was struck by the power of the human spirit, and its ability to endure.

That's how I felt with Lin, a woman I had worked with years before. She was a young Chinese woman who was in an arranged marriage. Lin spoke very little English and stayed at home raising her daughter. She was financially dependent on her husband, but he refused to give her any money even though he owned their home and a restaurant. If she needed to buy something, she would take money from the cash register and leave a note. Lin's husband started beating her on a regular basis. Whenever she would threaten to call the police, he would scream, "I am the law."

One day Lin was cooking lunch for their daughter in the restaurant. Her husband came over and threw the pot of boiling water into the sink. Lin had to feed her daughter so she went back to the sink, refilled the pot and put it back on the stove. When the water started to boil, her husband placed a ladle inside and threw the scalding water on Lin's back. Her skin was bubbling with second-degree burns. He did this in front of the kitchen workers who stood back, afraid to help her, afraid to lose their jobs.

When Lin first came to my office, she was so timid. Even with a translator, she kept her head down when answering my questions. All that

REFLECTIONS OF A DOMESTIC VIOLENCE PROSECUTOR

If we can transform one life, then our work is not in vain.

changed the day she testified in Supreme Court against her husband. There she was on the witness stand in open court before a judge and jury, facing her abuser, with everyone listening to what she had to say. In that courtroom she learned that her husband was no longer the law.

I remember walking down the front steps of the courthouse praising Lin for how courageous she was, and how well she had done on the witness stand. For the first time, she held her head high and was beaming with delight. The very act of testifying against her abuser had empowered her. The District Attorney's Office was able to connect Lin with an agency that provided a wide range of support services in her native language, including counseling and legal representation for divorce.

Lin eventually left New York with her daughter to start a new life, as her husband spent the next few years behind bars. I hear from Lin every few years. She is happy and thriving.

I offer these cases as examples of the system working, of victims being satisfied with the treatment they received, of juries holding perpetrators accountable, and of judges imposing sentences commensurate with the crime. This is the very reason prosecutors need to continue their efforts. If we can transform one life, then our work is not in vain.

Conclusion

AS THE CASES IN THIS BOOK illustrate, most battered women face systemic issues that are beyond the capabilities of the criminal justice system to resolve. While prosecution is an important component of effective domestic violence policy, making it the primary means for addressing domestic violence, and neglecting necessary reforms in education, job training, living wages, safe affordable housing, universal child care, reproductive choice, access to birth control and family planning, and the media's representation of women, will not bring about meaningful change for battered women.[249]

As Elizabeth Schneider has noted,

> Domestic violence is now treated as a problem in isolation, with neither history nor social context. It is viewed as though it can be "solved" or "treated" through legal remedies or mediation or therapy alone, without considering the issues of women's equality and gender subordination. In this way, the concept of battering has been unmoored from its historical roots of gender subordination and feminist activism.[250]

While there have been many advances for women over the past forty years, there are still mixed messages regarding women's rights and status.[251] For example, even though more women than men have received

In the end, social change for women has been about moving a few steps forward and then seeing a backlash taking us a few steps backward.

graduate education since the late 1990's,[252] popular culture continues to demean and objectify women, relying on regressive stereotypes to define them.[253] Despite equal levels of education, the gender wage gap persists, with men making more money than women.[254] Historic beliefs regarding female domesticity continue, with women doing more housework than men even in homes where both husband and wife work.[255]

The reality for poor women is more disturbing. While poverty rates for single mother households are high,[256] the federal government refuses to pay for abortion services for the poor.[257] Even if a woman manages to find the money to exercise her reproductive choice, the United States Supreme Court allows states to impose barriers, which effectively limit choice for poor women.[258]

And despite all the legislative, judicial and social advances for battered women since the 1970's, the United States Supreme Court in 2000, in *United States v. Morris*, refused to see domestic violence as a national problem.[259] By striking down the civil rights remedy of the Violence Against Women Act as an unconstitutional exercise of congressional power, the Supreme Court found that violence against women was merely an issue for the local police to resolve. But five years later, in *Town of Castle Rock v. Gonzalez*, the United States Supreme Court found that the police were not obligated to arrest a domestic violence offender who was in violation of an order of protection, even though the state had a mandatory arrest law.[260] In one fell swoop, the United Supreme Court undid forty years of battered women's advocacy by rendering mandatory arrest laws meaningless, leaving parties aggrieved by police inaction without a remedy.

CONCLUSION

Yet, there is hope for battered women in the international arena. After losing in the United States Supreme Court, Jessica Gonzalez brought her case to the Inter–American Commission on Human Rights. In 2011, the Commission found in favor of Ms. Gonzalez, holding that the United States violated her human rights by failing to act on her order of protection.[261]

In the end, social change for women has been about moving a few steps forward and then seeing a backlash taking us a few steps backward.[262] The suggestions I have laid out in this book will help move us forward. By addressing misogynistic beliefs in the media and schools, we can begin to change the thinking regarding the status of women. By creating flexible domestic violence prosecution policies and collaborative interdisciplinary response teams, battered women are more likely to trust the criminal justice system. By having a thorough screening process for the selection and monitoring of domestic violence judges, we can help ensure that the most qualified judges are handling these cases. By requiring judges to hold batterers accountable for their coercive and intimidating behavior during the pendency of a criminal case, the judiciary can send a strong message that such behavior won't be tolerated. By educating legislatures to the ways evidentiary rules limit justice for battered women, we can pave the way for new laws that ensure battered women's stories are heard in court. By funding global positioning systems and enacting bail statutes that consider safety, we can better respond to the dangers battered women face. And by funding a wide variety of services from housing, job training, medical and child care, to civil legal representation and Family Justice Centers, we can help ensure that we are adequately responding to the needs of battered women.

The sooner we implement these reforms, the quicker we can better the conditions for women in general and battered women in particular.

Endnotes

1. This is the term most often used to describe women who have been physically abused by an intimate partner. Unfortunately, the term tends to define women solely by the abuse, failing to capture their strength and resiliency. "Battered woman does not capture the range and complexity of a woman's experiences beyond the facts of abuse. The term makes her the problem, not her experiences. We reinforce this interpretation by talking about the 'problems of battered women,' rather than focusing on the problem of male violence or male battering of women, or men who assert and use violence as a means of control." Elizabeth M. Schneider, Battered Women and Feminist Lawmaking (New Haven: Yale University Press, 2002) 60–62.

2. Casey Gwinn, Dream Big: A Simple Complicated Idea to Stop Family Violence (Tucson: Wheatmark, 2010). See for a history of Family Justice Centers.

3. "The courtroom is the theater in which the dramas of battered women have been brought to public attention. Trials like that of Francine Hughes, whose story became the book and movie The Burning Bed, create a cultural and legal spotlight that has in some ways benefited women by increasing public knowledge of the existence of domestic violence. However, the press has emphasized sensational cases that have a high level of terrorism against women and a grotesque quality of abuse. These cases come to define a cultural image of domestic violence, and the women in these cases define an image of battered women." Martha Mahoney, "Legal Images of Battered Women: Redefining the Issue of Separation," Michigan Law Review 90, no.1 (1991): 4.

4. Elizabeth Pleck, Domestic Tyranny: The Making of American Social Policy Against Family Violence from Colonial Times to the Present (Champaign: University of Illinois, 1987).

5. "Although there were humanitarian and biblical dimensions to the Puritan legal code, the major purpose of their laws was to reinforce hierarchical relationships, either in the family or in society." Ibid., 25.

6. Reva B. Siegel, "The Rule of Love: Wife Beating as Prerogative," The Yale Law Journal 105 no. 8. (1996): 2117, 2122–2123.; Sally F. Goldfarb, "Violence Against Women and the Persistence of Privacy," Ohio State Law Journal 61 no. 1. (2000). See for an historical analysis of legal responses to domestic violence.
7. Pleck, Domestic Tyranny, 25.
8. Ibid.
9. Ibid., 23.
10. Ibid.
11. Ibid., 49–66.
12. Ibid., 56–60.
13. "Divorce for the drunkard's wife was a radical proposal, which some woman's rights leaders regarded as fundamental. They set forth the issue of divorce for the drunkard's wife as a conflict between the claims of the traditional male–dominated family and a woman's right to autonomy and personal safety. The vehemence of their rhetoric may have helped defeat divorce reform legislation." Ibid., 50.
14. Siegel, "The Rule of Love," 2162.
15. Ibid., 2129.
16. Ibid., 2154.
17. Ibid., 2158. Quoting *State v. Oliver*, 70 N.C. 60, 61–62 (1874).
18. Pleck, Domestic Tyranny, 55–56.
19. The biggest obstacle for battered women during the nineteen century was finding ways to keep their children and support themselves "in an economy of limited jobs for women, limited child care, and little or no reliable aid to single mothers....Moreover, these women of the past had the added burden of defying a social norm condemning marital separation and encouraging submission as a womanly virtue." Linda Gordon, Heroes of Their Own Lives: The Politics and History of Family Violence–Boston, 1880–1960 (Champaign: University of Illinois: 1988), 272.
20. Pleck, Domestic Tyranny, 151.
21. Ibid.,158–159.
22. Ibid., 7.
23. Ibid., 184.
24. Del Martin, Battered Wives (San Francisco: Glide Publications, 1976), 12–13.
25. Schneider, Battered Women and Feminist Lawmaking, 22–23.
26. Pleck, Domestic Tyranny, 183,199–200.
27. "There are multiple sources of controversy among family violence experts. First and most simply, public and scholarly attention to this violence has a relatively short history...It has been only during the past three decades that wife abuse... [has] been [a] specific topic[s] of concern, and most social service interventions have an even shorter history. Making sense of any social problem is difficult; something as complex as family violence cannot be understood, much less resolved, in the short span of a few decades. Regrettably, it is only in fiction–including that presented through the mass media–that human troubles are easily understood and quickly fixed." Donileen R. Loseke, Richard J. Gelles, and Mary M. Cavanaugh eds., Current Controversies on Family Violence (Thousand Oaks: Sage, 2005), xv.
28. Donileen R. Loseke, "Through a Sociological Lens: The Complexities of Family Violence," in Current Controversies in Family Violence, 35.

29 Donald G. Dutton and Mark Bodnarchuk, "Through a Psychological Lens: Personality Disorder and Spouse Assault," in Current Controversies in Family Violence, 5.
30 Kersti A. Yllo, "Through a Feminist Lens: Gender, Diversity and Violence: Extending the Feminist Framework," in Current Controversies in Family Violence, 19.
31 Evan Stark, Coercive Control: How Men Entrap Women in Personal Life (New York: Oxford University Press, 2007), 83–111. See for an analysis of various studies and findings.
32 Murray Straus, "Women's Violence Toward Men is a Serious Social Problem," in Current Controversies in Family Violence, 55.
33 Donileen R. Loseke and Demie Kurz, "Men's Violence Toward Women is the Serious Social Problem," in Current Controversies in Family Violence, 79.
34 Peggy Orenstein, Cinderella Ate My Daughter: Dispatches From The Front Lines Of The New Girlie–Girl Culture (New York: Harper Collins, 2011).; Sharon Lamb and Lyn Mikel Brown, Packaging Girlhood: Rescuing Our Daughters from Marketers' Schemes (New York: St. Martin's Griffin, 2007).; Jennifer Pozner, Reality Bites Back: The Troubling Truth about Guilty Pleasure TV (Berkely: Seal Press, 2010). Corporate media reap exorbitant profits by portraying women on reality television as desperate gold diggers who are brainless and catty.
35 Gale Dines, Pornland: How Porn has Hijacked Our Sexuality (Boston: Beacon Press, 2010).; Duke Nukem Forever, a video game produced by Gearbox Software, where the goal is to kidnap a "babe" and then slap her on the buttocks to calm her down when she screams in terror. See feministfatale.com/2011/03/rants-of-a-gamergirl-duke-nukem-smack-my-chick-up/.; "Hollywood likes to pretend it has grown up and taken its seat in corporate America. But it hasn't when it comes to violence toward women." David Carr, "Insulting Chuck Lorre, Not Abuse, Gets Sheen Sidelined," New York Times, February 28, 2011, www.nytimes.com/2011/02/28/business/media/28carr.html.
36 See e.g., "No Endz no Skinz" by Big L; "P.I.M.P." by 50 Cent; "Me and My Bitch" by Notorious BIG; "Area Codes" by Ludacris; "Bitches Ain't Shit" by Dr. Dre; See BET network videos; Byron Hurt documentary, Hip Hop: Beyond Beats and Rhymes (2006).
37 Psychologist Lenore E. Walker, in her groundbreaking work, The Battered Woman (New York: Harper & Row, 1979), interviewed over one hundred battered women in order to understand the psychological effects of battering. Dr. Walker coined the term "battered women's syndrome" to explain a set of behaviors resulting from repeated abuse, and found that many women develop learned helplessness, which interferes with their ability to leave violent relationships. Unfortunately, her theory has resulted in a stereotype that all battered women are helpless and timid. This stereotype has been

ENDNOTES

reinforced in popular culture with movies like The Burning Bed (1984) with Farrah Fawcett, and Sleeping with the Enemy (1991) with Julia Roberts, where they play passive battered women.
38 Lori S. Kohn, "Barriers to Reliable Credibility Assessments: Domestic Violence Victim Witnesses," American University Journal of Gender, Social Policy and the Law 11, no. 733 (2003).; Marian Meyers, News Coverage of Violence Against Women: Engendering Blame (Thousand Oaks: Sage, 1997). Female victims of violence are portrayed by the news media as either virgin/whore or good girl/bad girl so that women appear to be either innocent or to blame for the violence inflicted on them.; Anna Holmes, "The Disposable Woman," New York Times, March 3, 2011, nytimes.com/2011/03/04/opinion/04holmes.html. Hollywood's elevation of Charlie Sheen, despite his long history of abusing women, is the result of unsympathetic portrayal of his victims. Ex–wives were portrayed as gold–diggers, while ex–girlfriends, who were both porn actresses, were deemed to have gotten what they deserved.
39 National Coalition for Free Men, www.ncfm.org; RADAR–Respecting Accuracy in Domestic Abuse Reporting, www.mediaradar.org; Equal Justice Foundation, www.ejfi.org.
40 Jacquelyn C. Campbell and Jennifer Manganello, "Changing Public Attitudes as a Prevention Strategy to Reduce Intimate Partner Violence," Journal of Aggression, Maltreatment & Trauma 13, no. 3 (2006):

13–39.; "So while new laws can be vehicles for changing social attitudes, the persistence of these very social attitudes can impair the meaningful implementation of legal reforms." Schneider, Battered Women and Feminist Lawmaking, 189.
41 Martin, Battered Wives, 176.
42 National Conference of State Legislatures, www.ncsl.org/?tabid=17582#state.
43 Ibid.
44 Centers for Disease Control and Prevention, " Teen Dating Violence," (2010), http://www.cdc.gov/ViolencePrevention/intimatepartnerviolence/teen_dating_violence.html/.; Jan Hoffman, "A Warning to Teenagers Before They Start Dating," New York Times, May 6, 2012, www.nytimes.com/2012/06/04/us/middle–school–students–focus–of–anti–violence–effort.html?pagewanted=1&tntemail0=y&r=1&emc=tnt.
45 Orenstein, Cinderella Ate My Daughter.
46 See e.g, "British Schools to teach Domestic Violence: Children as Young as Five to Learn about Gender Equality," http://britishaffairs.suite101.com/article.cfm/british_schools_to_teach_domestic_violence; New Jersey legislation authorizes such education programs to begin in elementary school, N.J.S.A. 18A:35–4.23.
47 www.cadvny.org
48 ScenariosUSA.com
49 Ibid.
50 Bellbajo.org (Belbajo is Hindi for "ring the bell") It is a domestic violence awareness campaign in India urging citizens to ring the

bell if they hear fighting within a home.
51 "Campaigns designed only to raise awareness about a problem are often not successful." Campbell and Manganello, "Changing Public Attitudes," 30.; See, e.g., The Family Violence Prevention Fund, "There's No Excuse for Domestic Violence," "It's Your Business" and "Coaching Boys into Men," www.endabuse.org/section/campaigns/.; New York State Office for the Prevention of Domestic Violence, "You are not his property" and "it's No Game!," www.opdv.state.ny.us/public_awareness/campaigns/.
52 Meyers, Engendering Blame. Showing how news media needs to move away from a simplistic and sensational reporting style to one that provides a deeper contextualized analysis.
53 Campbell and Manganello, "Changing Public Attitudes," 23. "Soul City," was an innovative program used in South Africa in 1999 to address domestic violence, HIV, sexual harassment, and hypertension that consisted of a 13 part prime time serialized TV drama, a 45-part radio drama in 9 languages, and one million each of three information booklets to reach a large segment of the population.
54 Cesar Chelala, "Learning From Soap Operas," *New York Times*, April 4, 2010, www.nytimes.com/2010/06/04/opinion/04iht_edchelala.html.
55 Musician Ruth Gerson, in her 2011 album Deceived, tackles the way domestic violence is part of the fabric of our society, ruthgerson.com.; Paul Butler, Let's Get Free: A Hip–Hop Theory of Justice (New York: The New Press, 2009), 123–145. Discussing the power of hip–hop on culture and law.
56 www.bbc.co.uk/programmes/b00x923h.
57 "Abusers" is a reality television show due to air that follows abusers and victims. Format raises serious questions about safety to women profiled. See Jessica Wakeman, ""Abusers" Reality Show Brings Real–Life Domestic Violence Abusers Into Your Living Room," Ms. Magazine, July 20, 2010, http://msmagazine.com/blog/blog/2010/07/20/%E2%80%9Cabusers%E2%80%9D-reality-show-brings-real-life-domestic-violence-abusers-into-your-living-room/.
58 Leigh Goodmark, "When is a Battered Woman not a Battered Woman? When She Fights Back," Yale Journal of Law and Feminism 20, no. 75, (2008) 83. Describing the characteristics of the paradigmatic victim as one who is passive, submissive, and weak, and does not fight back.
59 N.Y. P.L. § 70.02.
60 N.Y. C.P.L. § 620.20.
61 Goodmark, "When is a Battered Woman Not a Battered Woman?."
62 Ibid.
63 Goodmark, "When is a Battered Woman Not a Battered Woman?," 77. Noting how in applications for civil protection orders, advocates have victims tailor their stories for fear judges won't believe them if they don't present as the stereotypical victim.; Laurie S. Kohn, "Barriers to Reliable Credibility Assessments," 735. Referring to this phenomenon as "demeanor re–packaging".

64 Goodmark, "When is a Battered Woman Not a Battered Woman?," 80. Battered women tell their narratives to many actors in the system. How the hearer interprets and constructs the story determines whether they will receive help.; Laurie S. Kohn, "Barriers to Reliable Credibility Assessments," 734. Victims who do not present on the witness stand as a paradigmatic victim—weak, passive and helpless—will not be believed by jury.; Melanie Randall, "Deconstructing The "Image" of the Battered Woman: Domestic Violence and the Construction of "Ideal Victims": Assaulted Women's "Image Problems" In Law," St. Louis University Public Law Review 23, no. 107 (2004).
65 Kohn "Barriers to Reliable Credibility Assessments," 742. Jurors and judges lack nuanced understanding of domestic violence and use preconceived notions to evaluate credibility.; Martha Mahoney, "Legal Images of Battered Women," 37. Judges and juries hear testimony of battered women through the filter of cultural stereotypes.
66 Schneider, Battered Women and Feminist Lawmaking, 78.
67 Pleck, Domestic Tyranny, 24–25.; Gordon, Heroes of Their Own Lives, 253.
68 Schneider, Battered Women and Feminist Lawmaking, 74–86.
69 "Portrayal of women as solely victims or agents is neither accurate nor adequate to explain the complex realities of women's lives." Ibid., 82.
70 New York City police will not forcibly evict someone who has been living at location for more than thirty days. See NYRPAPL §§ 853. In order to get George out, Betty needed to institute legal proceedings in Housing Court and serve George with the papers. George, however, had the right to live in the apartment until a judge ordered him out, which presented serious safety issues. Also, Betty couldn't financially afford to miss work to appear in Court.
71 "A woman's self–assertion may be prominent in some contexts of her life and virtually absent in others." Schneider, Battered Women and Feminist Lawmaking, 85.
72 N.Y.F.C.A. § 154–a.
73 *People v. Collins*, 290 A.D.2d 457 (2d Dep't 2002).
74 Betty Friedan, The Feminine Mystique (New York: W. W. Norton, 1963).
75 Straus, "Women's Violence Toward Men."
76 Loseke and Kurz, "Men's Violence Toward Women."
77 Stark, Coercive Control.
78 Straus, "Women's Violence Toward Men," 67, 71. Recognizing how "misogynists and apologists for male violence" have used findings to further their own agenda.
79 Loseke and Kurz, "Men's Violence Toward Women," 81, 92–93. Noting how New Hampshire reduced resources for a shelter, and funding for a shelter in Chicago was blocked, as a result of family violence studies finding women as violent as men.
80 Stark, Coercive Control.
81 Ibid., 103–104.
82 Ibid.
83 Michael Kimmel, "Male Victims of Domestic Violence: A Substantive and Methodological

Research Review," Report to the Equality Committee of the Department of Education and Science (2002), new.vawnet.org/Assoc_Files_VAWnet/GenderSymmetry.pdf.
84 "Landscape of unprovoked but premeditated female violence remains strangely unexplored," Sam Tanenhaus, "Violence That Art Didn't See Coming," *New York Times*, February 28, 2010, http://www.nytimes.com/2010/02/28/arts/28bishop.html?pagewanted=2&emc=etal.
85 Susan Weitzman, Not to People Like Us: Hidden Abuse in Upscale Marriages (New York: Basic Books, 2000).
86 See Pozner, Reality Bites Back.
87 Butler, Let's Get Free, 125.; Hurt, Hip Hop.
88 Sam Dillon, "Biden to Discuss New Guidelines about Campus Sex Crimes," *New York Times*, April 4, 2011, www.nytimes.com/2011/04/04/education/04violence.html?.; Maureen Dowd, "Their Dangerous Swagger," *New York Times*, June 9, 2010, www.nytimes.com/2010/06/09/opinion/09dowd.html. Teenage boys at a prestigious Washington DC area private school drafted teenage girls in a fantasy football like game where players scored points for sexual encounters with girls.; Juliet Macur, "At Virginia a Vigil and the First Attempts at Healing," *New York Times*, May 6, 2010, www.nytimes.com/2010/05/06/sports/06lacrosse.html?. Female college student brutally murdered by fellow student and ex-boyfriend who is from a prominent family.
89 Lisa W. Foderaro, "At Yale, Sharper Look at Treatment of Women," *New York Times*, April 8, 2011, www.nytimes.com/2011/04/08/nyregion/08yale.html?.
90 Pozner, Reality Bites Back, 16.
91 Ibid., 240, 242.
92 Ibid., 26–29.
93 Meyers, Engendering Blame.
94 "How real are reality TV catfights?," The Today Show, April 23, 2011, http://www.msnbc.msn.com/id/21134540/vp/42730522#42730522.
95 Susan Schechter, Women and Male Violence: The Visions and Struggles of the Battered Women's Movement (Cambridge: South End Press: 1982).
96 "Women abuse is viewed here as an historical expression of male domination manifested within the family and currently reinforced by the institutions, economic arrangements, and sexist division of labor within a capitalist society. Only by analyzing this total context of battering will women and men be able to devise a long range plan to eliminate it," Schecter, Women and Male Violence, 209.; Schneider, Battered Women and Feminist Lawmaking, 20–28.
97 Joan Zorza, "The Criminal Law of Misdemeanor Domestic Violence, 1970–1990," The Journal of Criminal Law and Criminology 83, no. 1 (1992): 46.
98 Ibid.
99 Schecter, Women and Male Violence, 177.
100 Ibid., 119. Quoting principals of Massachusetts Coalition of Battered Women's Services Groups.
101 Ibid., 113.

102 *Bruno v. Codd*, 90 Misc.2d 1047 (N.Y. Sup. Ct. 1977), rev'd in part, appeal dismissed in part, 47 N.Y.2d 582 (1979).; *Scott v. Hart*, No. C–76–2395 (N.D. Cal., filed Oct 28, 1976).; See also Zorza, "The Criminal Law of Misdemeanor Domestic Violence," 54. for a discussion of lawsuits.
103 Lawrence W. Sherman, Policing Domestic Violence: Experiments and Dilemmas (New York: Free Press, 1992).
104 Ibid., 91.
105 *Thurman v. City of Torrington*, 595 F. Supp. 1521 (1984).; See also Zorza, "The Criminal Law of Misdemeanor Domestic Violence," 60. for a discussion of lawsuit.
106 Zorza, "The Criminal Law of Misdemeanor Domestic Violence," 60.
107 Aya Gruber, "The Feminist War on Crime," Iowa Law Review 92 (2007): 741.
108 Attorney General's Task Force on Family Violence 1984.
109 See 42 U.S.C. 3796hh.
110 Sherman, Policing Domestic Violence.
111 Ibid., 125–153,185.
112 See National Institute of Justice, "Domestic Violence Cases: What Research Shows About Arrest and Dual Arrest Rates," (2008), http://www.ojp.usdoj.gov/nij/publications/dv-dual-arrest-222679/contents.htm. 22 states and the District of Columbia have mandatory arrest laws.
113 See Joan Zorza, "Must We Stop Arresting Batterers?: Analysis and Policy Implications of New Police Domestic Violence Studies," New England Law Review 28 (1994): 929.
114 Jean Ferguson, "Professional Discretion and the Use of Restorative Justice Programs in Appropriate Domestic Violence Cases: An Effective Intervention," Criminal Law Brief 4, no. 3 (2009): 8. Citing studies examining effects of prosecution on recidivism rates.; National Institute of Justice, "Batterer Intervention Programs: Where Do We Go From Here?," (2003), www.ojp.usdoj.gov/nij. Studies find little or no reduction in violence or attitudes from attendance in programs.
115 Cheryl Hanna, "No Right to Choose: Mandated Victim Participation in Domestic Violence Prosecutions," Harvard Law Review 109 (1996): 1849.
116 Ibid.
117 Tom Lininger, "Evidentiary Issues in Federal Prosecutions of Violence Against Women," Indiana Law Review 36, no. 687 (2003): note 76. Eighty to ninety percent of women do not want to proceed with criminal charges.
118 "The societal benefits gained through this criminal justice response to domestic violence far outweigh any short–term costs to women's autonomy and collective safety." Hanna, "No Right to Choose," 1857.; "Aggressive prosecution is the appropriate response to domestic violence cases for several reasons. First, domestic violence affects more that just the individual victim; it is a public safety issue that affects all of society. Second, prosecutors cannot rely upon domestic violence victims to appropriately vindicate the State's interests in holding batterers responsible for the crimes they commit because

victims often decline to press charges. Third, prosecutors must intervene to protect victims and their children and to prevent batterers from further intimidating their victims and manipulating the justice system." Donna Wills, "Mandatory Prosecution in Domestic Violence Cases: Domestic Violence: The Case for Aggressive Prosecution," UCLA Women's Law Journal 7 (1997): 173.; Casey Gwinn, J.D. & Sgt. Anne O'Dell, "Domestic Violence and Child Abuse: Stopping the Violence: The Role of the Police Officer and the Prosecutor," Western State University Law Review 20 (1993): 297.

119 "The problem with policies like mandatory arrest is that they reify two goals—safety and perpetrator accountability—and marginalize autonomy, serving women who share the goals of the system but disenfranchising those with divergent goals." Leigh Goodmark, "Autonomy Feminism: An Anti-Essentialist Critique of Mandatory Interventions in Domestic Violence Cases," Florida State University Law Review 37, no. 1, (2009): 4.; Linda Mills, "Killing Her Softly: Intimate Abuse and the Violence of State Intervention," Harvard Law Review 113 (1999): 550.

120 Goodmark, "Autonomy Feminism,"; Mills, "Killing Her Softly,"; Donna Coker, "Crime Control and Feminist Law Reform in Domestic Violence Law: A Critical Review," Buffalo Criminal Law Review 4 (2001): 801.; Deborah Weissman, "The Personal is Political—and Economic: Rethinking Domestic Violence," Brigham Young University Law Review 387 (2007).; Laurie Kohn, "The Justice System and Domestic Violence: Engaging the Case But Divorcing the Victim," New York University Review of Law and Social Change 32 (2008): 191.

121 Kristian Miccio, "A House Divided: Mandatory Arrest, Domestic Violence and the Conservatization of the Battered Women's Movement," Houston Law Review 42 (2005): 237. (co-author of New York state's mandatory arrest law).

122 "While battering is a phenomenon of gender subordination, it may also be a function of racism, poverty, and conquest. If feminist anti-domestic violence work is to be liberatory, it must recognize the importance of these intersections in women's lives. Ignoring the importance of these oppressive structures in the lives of battered women results in interventions that ultimately fail the women whose lives are most affected by those structures: poor women and women of color." Donna Coker, "Enhancing Autonomy for Battered Women: Lessons from Navajo Peacemaking," UCLA Law Review 47 (1999): 1, 11.; "By focusing solely on the criminal justice system and criminal sanctions, other aspects of communal life that contribute to the perpetuation of male intimate violence remain unexamined—and accountable." Miccio, "A House Divided," 290.

123 Goodmark, "Autonomy Feminism."; Miccio, "A House Divided."

124 Leigh Goodmark, "The Legal Response to Domestic Violence: Problems and Possibilities: Law is the Answer? Do We Know that For Sure?," St. Louis University Public Law Review 23, no. 7 (2004): 35.; Coker, "Enhancing Autonomy for Battered Women."
125 National Institute of Justice, "Domestic Violence Cases: What Research Shows About Arrest and Dual Arrest Rates," (2008), http://www.ojp.usdoj.gov/nij/publications/dv-dual-arrest-222679/ch1/findings.htm#three. Arrest rates in intimate partner cases are 97% higher in states with mandatory arrest laws compared to states with discretionary laws.; Emily Sack, "Battered Women and the State: The Struggle for the Future of Domestic Violence Policy," Wisconsin Law Review (2004): 1657.
126 Miccio, "A House Divided," 284–285.
127 The domestic violence incident involving David Johnson, an aide to former New York State Governor David Patterson, is illustrative. Johnson choked his girlfriend, ripped off her clothing, and shoved her into a dresser. The victim's 911 call was placed third in line, after a traffic crash and dispute between a landlord and tenant. When the officers finally responded, they classified the incident as harassment, a non–criminal offense. However, the facts of the case supported numerous misdemeanor charges, which would have mandated arrest under New York State's mandatory arrest law, unless the victim requested otherwise. Whether intentionally or inadvertently, officers still fail to handle these cases properly. To abandon mandatory arrest policies in favor of discretionary one's would be extremely problematic. See Ailsa Chang, "NYPD Reviewing Response to Domestic Violence Call Involving Governor's Aide," WNYC, August 23, 2010, http://www.wnyc.org/articles/wnyc-news/2010/aug/23/nypd-reviewing-response-domestic-violence-call-involving-governors-aide/.
128 "Although prosecutors, the judiciary, and probation offices must all play a role in protecting women from abusive partners, it is the role of the police, who are the first to respond, that usually determines whether victims ever get to a courthouse. Police are the actors who must decide whether to arrest the abuser or to tell the victim about her rights. Without police help, few victims will even realize what their options are." Zorza, "The Criminal Law of Misdemeanor Domestic Violence," 60.; Barbra Hart, "Arrest: What's the Big Deal," William and Mary Journal of Women and Law 3 (1997): 207.
129 "Certainly, domestic violence is a crime against the state and generally should be treated as such; but victim advocates could be a key to transforming one–size–fits–all prosecution policies into responses that are also tailored to the concerns of individual women." Deborah Epstein, "Effective Intervention in Domestic Violence Cases: Rethinking the Roles of Prosecutors, Judges, and the Court System," Yale Journal of Law and Feminism 11, no. 3 (1999): 20.; "[T]o craft a

one-size-fits-all solution is deeply problematic because it fails to account for the varied conditions that shape women's lives and responses." Miccio, "A House Divided," 305.; "[I]t is also important to allow battered women to identify their goals, and to listen carefully when they do." Jane Murphy, "Engaging with the State: The Growing Reliance on Lawyers and Judges to Protect battered Women," Journal of Gender, Social Policy and the Law 11, no. 2 (2003): 514.; "[W]omen's decisions whether or not to support criminal intervention are often related to whether or not they can afford to prioritize prosecution over other more immediate concerns such as food, employment, and childcare." Coker, "Crime Control and Feminist Law Reform in Domestic Violence Law," 823.

130 For the past few years, I have approached my cases this way and have encountered satisfaction from a number of women who initially did not want to pursue criminal prosecution. While I did not drop charges, I worked out plea agreements to misdemeanor crimes with sentences of probation and limited orders of protection as opposed to felony pleas with prison time and full stay away orders. Noteworthy is the fact that when there were subsequent incidents of abuse, the women either called me or the social worker for help. Whereas in the past, when I ignored what women were saying, I usually never heard from them again.

131 See note 114 above.

132 Lisa Goodman and Deborah Epstein, Listening to Battered Women, A Survivor Centered Approach to Advocacy, Mental Health, and Justice (Washington DC: American Psychological Association, 2008). Social support is critical for women in abusive relationships.

133 Epstein, "Effective Intervention in Domestic Violence Cases," 19. Cases exist on a spectrum and weight accorded to a victim's decision not to prosecute should reflect financial, familial and emotional connection to offender.

134 "If we care about victims, our ultimate goal must be their safety—a goal that is most effectively served by providing victims with the best possible interaction with the system so that when they are ready to leave the relationship, they know where to seek assistance and that they will be treated with respect." Kohn, "The Justice System and Domestic Violence," 246.

135 See e.g. Ferguson, "Professional Discretion and the Use of Restorative Justice Programs in Appropriate Domestic Violence Cases."; Laurie Kohn, "What's So Funny About Peace, Love, and Understanding? Restorative Justice as a New Paradigm for Domestic Violence Intervention," Seton Hall Law Review 40 (2010): 517.

136 Ferguson, "Professional Discretion and the Use of Restorative Justice Programs in Appropriate Domestic Violence Cases," 11. Quoting Tony F. Marshall, Restorative Justice: An Overview, A Report by the Home Office (1999): 5.

137 Coker, "Enhancing Autonomy for Battered Women." Discussing need for domestic violence

interventions that address specific needs of women.
138 See note 135 above.
139 Cheryl Hanna, "The Paradox of Hope: The Crime and Punishment of Domestic Violence," William and Mary Law Review 39 (1998): 1505, 1506. Referring to the criminal justice system's oft-used expression justifying pursuit of a criminal case.
140 Lawyers on the American Bar Association's Commission on Domestic Violence Listserv compiled these training exercises. (On file with author).
141 Ann Jones, Next Time She'll be Dead: Battering and How to Stop It (Boston: Beacon Press,1994).
142 "Low income women may not be able to afford the arrest and prosecution of their partners; the economic resources their partners provide might be more important than a cessation of the battering at a particular point in time." Goodmark, "Autonomy Feminism," 38.
143 Jane Murphy, "Engaging with the State," 511. Low income and childcare issues can be barriers for women to partake in time consuming nature of criminal justice system.
144 In New York state, when the police respond to a domestic violence incident they are required to fill out a pre-printed form known as a Domestic Incident Report. N.Y.C.P.L. § 140.10(5).
145 "Because of the complexity of battering relationships, victims experience a wide range of pressures and emotions in the aftermath of a violent episode. These forces compel most victims to perceive battering relationships in shades of gray that do not exist in the monochrome world of most lawyers, police officers, and judges. While some victims may wholeheartedly and consistently embrace the actor's mission to end the relationship, most victims will, at some point during a criminal or civil case, deviate from the path to a successful termination of the relationship." Kohn, "The Justice System and Domestic Violence," 200–201.
146 But see Goodmark, "Autonomy Feminism," 46., arguing that the criminal justice system should allow women to make their own choices regarding criminal prosecution even if that means further danger or even death.
147 Hanna, "No Right to Choose," 1908–1909. History of abuse and the seriousness of the offense are important criteria for prosecutor in determining whether to pursue charges.
148 Hanna, "The Paradox of Hope."
149 See e.g., note 146 above.
150 Hanna, "No Right to Choose," 1876.
151 See Part III below.
152 Kimberle Crenshaw, "Mapping the Margins: Intersectionality, Identity Politics, and Violence Against Women of Color," Stanford Law Review 43 (1991): 1241. Domestic violence policy can't just address violence inflicted by batterer but must also confront other multilayered issues that prevent women from leaving abusive relationships.; Criminalization is only one of many strategies to consider. "Far more important and more challenging is the need for state and state-supported resources to deal with real problems

battered women face—child care, shelters, welfare, work and workplace violence—and thus make it possible for women to have the economic and social independence that is a prerequisite to women's freedom from abuse." Schneider, Battered Women and Feminist Lawmaking, 196.

153 For legislative history of VAWA, see Sally Goldfarb, "The Civil Rights Remedy of the Violence Against Women Act: Legislative History, Policy Implications & Litigation Strategy: A Panel Discussion," Journal of Law and Policy 4, no. 391, (1996): 392–399.; See also, Joseph Biden, "Domestic Violence: A Crime, Not a Quarrel," (1993). Former Chair of the Senate Judiciary Committee and sponsor of the Violence Against Women Act addressing scope of crisis and justification for federal legislation.

154 Centers for Disease Control and Prevention, "Understanding Intimate Partner Violence," (2012), http://www.cdc.gov/violenceprevention/pdf/ipv_factsheet-a.pdf.

155 Centers for Disease Control and Prevention, "Intimate Partner Violence: Consequences," (2010), http://www.cdc.gov/violenceprevention/intimatepartnerviolence/consequences.html.

156 See grant programs administered by the Office on Violence Against Women of the United States Department of Justice, http://www.ovw.usdoj.gov/ovwgrantprograms.htm.; In order to qualify for grant funding, states must certify that laws or official policies encourage arrest, 42 U.S.C. § 3796hh.

157 Cheryl Hanna, "The Paradox of Hope." Discussing the need for interdisciplinary research to find out causes of battering and thus most effective punishment for domestic violence offenders.

158 N.Y.P.L. § 140.30(2). For this charge, a person must break into a home and cause physical injury to a non—participant.

159 "[O]ur criminal justice system is based on the proposition that individuals are tried only for the crime charged—not for who they are. Therefore, a ban exists on character evidence which demonstrates only that the defendant is a bad person. We forbid the jury to reason that if a person has committed previous assaults, he is the type of person who would assault the victim on this occasion, even though such propensity based reasoning is clearly logical." Myrna Raeder, "People v. Simpson: Perspectives on the Implication for the Criminal Justice System: The Admissibility of Prior Acts of Domestic Violence: Simpson and Beyond," Southern California Law Review 69 (1996): 1463, 1488–1489.

160 Stark, Coercive Control, 5.

161 Ibid., 92. Criminal law assumes "abuse consists of discrete acts that can be sharply delineated and so managed within a tight temporal frame, like stranger assaults."

162 "A new body of criminal and civil law is needed to identify coercive control as a public wrong. At a minimum, the new statutes would define coercive control as a course of conduct crime…" Stark, Coercive Control, 382.; "Laws

applied to prosecute domestic violence have a narrow temporal lens and a limited conception of harm. Together, these paradigms obscure defining aspects of battering: ongoing patterns of power and control are not addressed: nor is the full measure of injury that these patterns inflict redressed." Deborah Tuerkheimer, "Recognizing and Remedying the Harm of Battering: A Call to Criminalize Domestic Violence," Journal of Criminal Law and Criminology 94 (2004): 959, 970–971.; "Outside the realm of criminal law, social scientists almost universally describe domestic violence as an ongoing pattern of conduct motivated by the batterers desire for power and control over the victim. In contrast, the criminal statutes used to prosecute domestic violence almost universally describe discrete acts, without reference to the actor's motivation or other culpable acts." Alafair S. Burke, "Domestic Violence as a Crime of Pattern and Intent: An Alternative Reconceptualization," George Washington Law Review 75 (2007): 552, 555.
163 See Tom Lininger, "Evidentiary Issues."
164 Sarah Buel, "Putting Forfeiture to Work," U.C. Davis Law Review 43 (2010): 1295, 1322. Witness tampering is the most common crime committed by batterers.
165 "[B]efore law fully translates coercive control, it is important to consider whether, in doing so, it may simply reinforce questions about women's own agency and complicity in the abuse. Herein lies the central paradox of coercive control. By shifting the focus away from violence towards the broader dynamic of coercive control, we may be, albeit unintentionally, refocusing the law on the central question of "why didn't she leave?"" Cheryl Hanna, "The Paradox of Progress: Translating Evan Stark's Coercive Control into Legal Doctrine for Abused Women," Violence Against Women 15, no. 12 (2009): 1458–1476.
166 Sarah Buel, "Fifty Obstacles to Leaving, a.k.a., Why Abuse Victims Stay," Colorado Law Review 28 (1999): 19, 20.; "Sex role socialization, economic dependency, and unsupportive institutions combine to make the task of leaving an abusive relationship particularly difficult." Schechter, Women and Male Violence, 232.
167 Hanna, "The Paradox of Progress."
168 Kohn, "The Justice System and Domestic Violence," 247. Criminal justice system should focus on the way coercion profoundly influences victim's participation.
169 *Davis v. Washington*, 547 U.S. 813 (2006).; *Giles v. California*, 128 S. Ct. 2678 (2008).
170 Pursuant to the Confrontation Clause, defendants have the right to cross–examine witnesses against them. The confrontation clause limits the use of hearsay statements, which are out of court statements not subject to cross–examination.
171 "[W]hen defendants seek to undermine the judicial process by procuring or coercing silence from witnesses and victims, the Sixth Amendment does not require courts to acquiesce.

While defendants have no duty to assist the State in proving their guilt, they do have the duty to refrain from acting in ways that destroy the integrity of the criminal-trial system. [T]he rule of forfeiture by wrongdoing ...extinguishes confrontation claims on essentially equitable grounds. That is, one who obtains the absence of a witness by wrongdoing forfeits the constitutional right to confrontation." *Davis*, 547 U.S. at 833; See also, Deborah Tuerkheimer, "The Confrontation Clause: Forfeiture after Giles: The Relevance of "Domestic Violence Context,"" Lewis & Clark Law Review 13 (2009): 711.

172 See *People v Byrd*, 51 A.D.3d 267 (1st Dep't 2008). Defendant, who had a long history of physically abusing his girlfriend, beat her severely, severing her pancreas. While the victim testified in the grand jury, she refused to testify at trial. The appellate court upheld the trial court's admission of the victim's grand jury testimony under the theory of forfeiture by wrongdoing. The court held that the defendant's 400 plus telephone calls to victim while incarcerated, where he professed his love and requested forgiveness, was merely a tactic to control the victim and get her not to cooperate in the criminal prosecution.; See also *People v. Jernigan*, 41 A.D.3d 331 (1st Dep't 2007). Affirming admission of grand jury minutes at trial after finding defendant wrongfully made use of his relationship with girlfriend/victim in order to pressure her to violate her duty to testify against him.; *People v. Santiago*, 2003 Misc. Lexis 829 (S.

Ct. N.Y. County 2003). Trial court admitted grand jury testimony after evidence established that the defendant, who had a long history of abusing girlfriend, called her over 100 hundred times from jail thereby making her unavailable for trial.

173 Stark, Coercive Control, 5.
174 "Intimidation, isolation and control... is unique to men's abuse of women and is critical to explaining why women become entrapped in abusive relationships..." Stark, Coercive Control, 102.; See also Andrew King-Ries, "Forfeiture by Wrongdoing: A Panacea for Victimless Domestic Violence Prosecutions," Creighton Law Review 39 (2006): 441, 460. Battering relationship is a form of forfeiture by wrongdoing in that the batterer establishes and maintains relationship through criminal conduct designed to keep victim from reporting abuse to the authorities.
175 As a prior felony offender, Higgins faced between 8 and 12 years imprisonment on Burglary in the First Degree, a B felony offense. N.Y. P.L. § 70.06(6). However, because Beth refused to testify, I pleaded the case down two counts to Attempted Burglary in the Second Degree, a D felony offense, which carried a sentence between 3 and 7 years, and gave Higgins the minimum as an incentive to take the plea. N.Y. P.L. § 70.06(6).
176 See Diane L. Rosenfeld, and Kirstin Scheffler, "GPS Monitoring Systems for Batterers: Exploring a New Paradigm of Offender Accountability and Victim/Survivor Safety," Domestic

Violence Report, 12, no. 4 (2007). Discussing recent GPS legislation in Massachusetts.; See also, Ariana Green, "More States Use GPS to Track Abusers," *New York Times*, May 9, 2009, www.nytimes.com/2009/05/09/us/09gps.html.; "GPS to Warn Domestic Violence Victims," NPR, August 8, 2008, http://www.npr.org/templates/story/story.php?storyid=93420266.
177 N.Y. P.L. § 70.45.
178 See, "Greater Newburyport High Risk Response Team Safety and Accountability Report (2006–2008)," http://www.jeannegeigercrisiscenter.org/high-risk-case-teams. Although a small sample, none of the domestic violence offenders monitored by GPS, both pre-trial and post-conviction, had violated conditions during two-year period; GPS Monitoring Technologies and Domestic Violence: An Evaluation Study, *http:/www.ncjrs.gov/pdffiles1/nij/grants/238910.pdf*. Study found pre-trial use of GPS to monitor domestic violence offenders impacted both short and long term behavior.
179 "GPS Monitoring of Sex Offenders Should Be Used as Tool, Not Control Mechanism, Researchers Find," Science Daily, August 8, 2011, www.sciencedaily.com/releases/2011/08/110808152417.htm?utm_source=rss1.0&ut. Recent study at Sam Houston State University found that because of technological problems, GPS should be used as a tool, not a control mechanism.
180 See iSECUREtrac Corporation, http://www.isecuretrac.com, a technology company that provides Global Positioning Systems to law enforcement.
181 See, Massachusetts; Indiana; Kentucky: Minnesota; Illinois; Hawaii Connecticut; Florida; Michigan; Louisiana; Washington; Utah; New Hampshire; Colorado; Oklahoma; New Jersey, Electronic Monitoring Resource Center, https://emresourcecenter.nlectc.du.edu.
182 iSECUREtrac, "Domestic Violence," http://www.isecuretrac.com/solutions.aspx?p=domesticviolence.
183 Ibid.
184 Raeder, "People v. Simpson."; See also Federal Rule of Evidence § 404(b). Federal codification of prior bad acts evidence used by many states.; *People v. Molineux*, 168 N.Y. 264 (1901). Common law doctrine of prior bad acts evidence followed in New York.
185 Ibid.
186 See, Pamela Vartabedian, "The Need to Hold Batterers Accountable: Admitting Prior Acts of Abuse in Cases of Domestic Violence," Santa Clara Law Review 47 (2007): 157. California and Alaska are the only states with legislation allowing for admission of prior acts of domestic violence at trial for propensity.; Andrea Kovach, "Prosecutorial use of Other Acts of Domestic Violence for Propensity Purposes: A Brief Look at it's Past, Present, and Future," University of Illinois Law Review (2003): 1115. Explaining why justice in domestic violence cases demands that the prior history of abuse be admissible on the prosecution's case-in-chief.; Lisa Marie De Sanctis, "Bridging the Gap

187 Between the Rules of Evidence and Justice for Victims of Domestic Violence," Yale Journal of Law and Feminism 8 (1996): 359.
187 "In domestic violence cases, jurors obligated to sit in judgment are presented with a narrative warped by law. The verdicts that they reach may reflect this failing." Tuerkheimer, "Recognizing and Remedying the Harm of Battering," 988.
188 Stark, Coercive Control, 93–94. Criminal justice system treats incidents of domestic abuse as discrete acts yet "single most important characteristic of woman battering is that the weight of multiple harms is borne by the same person, giving abuse a cumulative effect that is far greater than the mere sum of its parts."
189 Ibid.
190 N.Y. C.P.L. § 510.30.
191 Karen Rooney, "Detaining For Danger Under the Federal and Massachusetts Bail Statutes: Controversial but Constitutional," New England Journal on Criminal and Civil Confinement 22 (1996): 465.
192 Ibid.
193 Under federal law, a judge must consider both risk of flight and dangerousness, and may impose conditions including electronic monitoring. If no condition of bail can assure the safety of the victim or community, then a judge can order preventative detention, 18 U.S.C. § 3142.
194 Karen Rooney, "Detaining for Danger," note 7.
195 See e.g., 725 ILCS 5/110–5.1.; Ala. Code § 15–13–190.; Minn. Laws § 629.72.; Fla. Stat. § 741.2902.; Carolyn Ham, "State Legislative Approaches to Bail or Pretrial Release Conditions for Domestic Violence Offenders," Battered Women's Justice Project (2004), http://www.bwjp.org/articles/article-list.aspx?mid=46.
196 In June of 2012, legislation (Senate Bill Number 7638/ Assembly Bill Number 10624) allowing the judiciary, when setting bail in cases of domestic violence, to consider whether the offender has a history of violating orders of protection and using or possessing firearms, passed both houses of the New York State Legislature. This legislation is expected to be delivered to Governor Cuomo and signed into law before the end of the year.
197 Jacquelyn C. Campbell, et al., "Risk Factors for Femicide in Abusive Relationships: Results From a Multisite Case Control Study," American Journal of Public Health 93, no. 7 (2003). As a result of studies like this, prosecutors in my office ask victims a series of questions to determine if lethality factors are present.
198 See e.g, 18 U.S.C. § 3147. Provision mandates consecutive sentence if a person commits a new offense while out on bail.; 18 U.S.C. § 3142 (c)(B)(xi). Judge can execute agreement with the defendant whereby he forfeits property if he fails to return to court.
199 "At least some of legal systems deficient handling of domestic violence cases derives from ignorance of dynamics of abusive relationships..." Buel, "Putting Forfeiture to Work," 1322.
200 See e.g. Nicole Fuller, "Judge Marries Defendant to

Alleged Victim," Baltimore Sun, March 18, 2010, http://www.baltimoresun.com/news/maryland/baltimore-county/bal-md.judge18mar18,0,2455093.story. Judge presiding over domestic violence trial marries defendant and victim so victim could assert marital privilege and not testify against defendant.; Gwen Filosa, "Domestic Violence Defendant Acquitted Despite Video Evidence," The Times–Picayune, April 14, 2010, http://www.nola.com/crime/index.ssf/2010/04/domestic_violence_defendant_ac.html. Judge acquits domestic violence defendant despite video capturing abuse because angry at district attorney for transferring domestic violence cases to criminal court from municipal court.; "One cannot underestimate the significance of misogynist judicial discourse… When defendant, court personnel and members of public hear such blatant victim blaming, cultural norms accepting interpersonal violence are reinforced." Buel, "Putting Forfeiture to Work," 1336.

201 Greg Berman & John Feinblatt, Good Courts: The Case for Problem Solving Justice (New York: The New Press, 2005). See for a discussion of domestic violence courts.

202 See e.g. NYC Mayor's Advisory Committee on the Judiciary, http://www.nyc.gov/html/acj/html/home/home.shtml; New York State Judicial Screening Committees, http://www.state.ny.us/governor/judicial/rules.html; Independent Judicial Election Qualification Commissions, http://www.ny-ijeqc.org.

203 See e.g., Professor John Feerick et al, "Commission to Promote Public Confidence in Judicial Elections," 17, http://www.courts.state.ny.us/reports/judiicaleletcionsreport.pdf. Recommending that in addition to members of the judiciary and the bar, academics and non-profit organizations take part in selection process of panel members screening elective judges to make it a more diverse and less partisan process.

204 See Stark, Coercive Control; Kohn, "The Justice System and Domestic Violence," 250. Judges need to understand coercion in a more nuanced way and ask questions to discover true motivations behind requests to lift orders of protection.

205 Buel, "Fifty Obstacles to Leaving."; See also, *Vermont v. Brillon*, 129 S. Ct. 1283 (2009). Court overruled Supreme Court of Vermont, finding defendant, a habitual domestic violence offender who sought to have his conviction thrown out on speedy trial grounds, was directly responsible for three year delay as he went through six lawyers, firing one who refused to "trash" the victim, while threatening to kill another.; "Unless one understands Stark's paradigm of coercive control, Brillon's actions seemed reasonable and benevolent de–contexualized from underlying issue of men's abuse of women. Yet, viewed from Stark's perspective, Brillon's actions are understood as strategic coercion, intended to deprive victim of her liberty and autonomy. She is still being

abused even though she is no longer beat or raped." Hanna, "The Paradox of Progress."; "[W]hat many women find is that the legal system itself becomes the batterer's forum for terrorizing his victim, and judges and others often give him the tools to perpetuate the abuse." Leigh Goodmark "The Legal Response to Domestic Violence."

206 William Glaberson, "Abuse Suspects, Your Calls Are Taped, Speak Up," *New York Times*, February 26, 2011, http://www.nytimes.com/2011/02/26/nyregion/26tapes.html?ref=todayspaper. Even though they are informed that their conversations are being recorded, batterers repeatedly call victims from jail in violation of no contact orders of protection. Typically, they are loving and contrite expressing interest in the day to day lives of their victims as well as the children in order to manipulate them out of testifying. It is not uncommon to hear batterers say, "If you drop the charges, I'll leave you alone" or "If you drop the charges, we can be together as a family."; http://researchnews.osu.edu/archives/vicrecant.htm. Recent study examining jail house phone calls found that batterers, through emotional appeals, influence victims' decision not to follow through on criminal prosecution.

207 See, "Greater Newburyport High Risk Response Team." Team consists of law enforcement, victim advocates and local hospitals in developing individual intervention plans.

208 "Community response efforts are limited to coordinating the procedural aspects of the cases and the resources available to victims. They are not designed to facilitate a coordinated effort among system actors that is individually tailored to the needs of any particular battered women." Lisa Goodman and Deborah Epstein, Listening to Battered Women, 87.

209 "Studies have revealed that interventions by one professional without input from other disciplines are rarely successful in protecting women and that in fact, they may actually put women at higher risk of re-abuse." Kohn, "The Justice System and Domestic Violence," 249.

210 Goodman and Epstein, Listening to Battered Women, 75. Criminal prosecution alone is not responsive to needs of women with multiple complex problems.

211 See e.g, N.Y. Mental Hygiene Law § 9.60. also known as Kendra's Law. Under certain circumstances a judge can mandate a mentally ill person into outpatient treatment and require they take psychiatric medications.

212 Goodman and Epstein, Listening to Battered Women, 64. Recovery for battered women requires strong social support network.

213 Amanda Hilt and Lynn McLain, "Stop the Killing: Potential Courtroom Use of a Questionnaire that predicts the Likelihood that a Victim of Intimate Partner Violence will Be Murdered by Her Partner," Wisconsin Journal of Law, Gender, and Society 24 (2009): 277.; David Adams, Why Do They Kill? Men Who

Murder Their Intimate Partners (Nashville: Vanderbilt University Press, 2007), 6.
214 Jacquelyn C. Campbell, et al., "Risk Factors for Femicide in Abusive Relationships: Results From a Multi–Site Case Control Study," American Journal of Public Health 93, no. 7 (2003). Authors interviewed 220 proxies for women killed by intimate parters and 343 survivors of intimate abuse in 11 cites to examine risk factors for femicide in abusive relationships.; Adams, Why Do They Kill?, 2,10. Author interviewed 31 wife killers and 39 female survivors of intimate partner violence to learn more about risk factors for femicide.
215 Campbell, "Risk Factors for Femicide."; Adams, Why Do They Kill?.
216 Adams, Why Do They Kill?, 259.
217 Adams, Why Do They Kill?, 6–7.; National Institute of Justice, "Practical Implications of Current Domestic Violence Research: For Law Enforcement, Prosecutors and Judges: Do the widely used risk instruments accurately predict re–abuse?," (2009): 26, www.ojp.usdoj.gov/nij.
218 National Institute of Justice, "Are victims accurate predictors of re–abuse?," (2009): 24.
219 See e.g The Lethality Assessment Program–Maryland Model, an intervention tool used by law enforcement, health care providers, the clergy and social workers to connect high–risk victims of domestic violence with service providers. Maryland Network Against Domestic Violence. www.mnadv.org.
220 Lundy Bancroft, Why Does He Do That? Inside the Minds of Angry and Controlling Men (New York: Berkely Books, 2002). The author, who worked with over 2000 abusive men, illustrates how batterers' behavior is based on beliefs and attitudes about women and how difficult it is for them to change.
221 National Institute of Justice, "Which abusers are most likely to try to kill their victims?," 26.; National Institue of Justice, "Men who Murder their Families: What the research tells us," http://www.ojp.usdoj.gov/nij/multimedia/video-men-who-murder.htm. Explaining and understanding domestic violence is one thing; predicting domestic violence homicides is quite another.
222 Martha Mahoney, "Legal Images of Battered Women." Coining the term "Separation Assault."
223 See Part III.
224 Adams, Why Do They Kill?, 81.
225 Ibid.
226 Ibid., 6. Since threats to kill far exceed the number of killings, it is difficult to know which cases are truly cause for concern.
227 N.Y. C.P.L. § 380.
228 "Killing one's partner communicates not only the ultimate act of control but also of ownership since one prerogative of ownership is to destroy that which is no longer of use to us." Adams, Why Do They Kill?, 254.; "The sense of ownership is one reason why abuse tends to get worse as relationships get more serious. The more history and commitment that develop in the couple, the more the abuser comes to think of his partner as a prized object. Possessiveness is at the core of the abuser's mind–set, the spring from which all the

other streams spout; on some level he feels that he owns you and therefore has the right to treat you as he sees fit." Bancroft, Why Does He Do That?, 73.
229 See note 215 above.
230 Adams, Why Do They Kill?, 7. Victims, for a variety of reasons, may fail to disclose certain risk factors making risk assessments unreliable.
231 Ibid., 261.
232 "The idyllic opening is part of almost every abusive relationship. How else would an abuser ever have a partner?" Bancroft, Why Does He Do That?, 110.
233 Ibid., 86. Describing some batterers as "drill sergeants" who are fanatically jealous, verbally assaulting partners with accusations of cheating. They control all aspects of a woman's life from what she can wear to who she can spend time with.
234 Adams, Why Do They Kill?, 29. Batterers avoid responsibility for violence by blaming the victim.
235 "Our research suggests that killers denigrate and blame their partners even more than abusers who don't kill. Perhaps the most surprising single finding about these men was how much rage they still held toward women they had killed." Ibid., 30.
236 Ibid.
237 Ibid., 81.
238 Ibid., 259.
239 See Part III.
240 Ibid.
241 See Casey Gwinn, Dream Big.
242 New York City Mayor's Office to Combat Domestic Violence, *www.nyc.gov/html/ocdv/html/fjc/fjc.shtml*. See for information on the Brooklyn Family Justice Center.
243 Amy K. Glasmeier, "Living Wage Calculator," Poverty in America, *www.livingwage.geog.psu.edu/*. While minimum wage is $7.25 an hour, a living wage for a single mother and child in New York City is $19.66.
244 Ask the DA, "Domestic Violence," Brooklyn Eagle, www.Brooklyneagle.com/categories/category.php?category-id=4&id=41967.
245 Martin, Battered Wives, 123–124.
246 Meyers, Engendering Blame.
247 See note 70 above.
248 Rape in the First Degree and Sodomy in the First Degree are both B felony offenses carrying a sentence ranging between 5 and 25 years' imprisonment. N.Y.P.L. § 70. The judge sentenced the defendant to concurrent terms of imprisonment on each count.
249 Tough domestic violence laws are meaningless if government policies make young women vulnerable to victimization. Texas, for example, passed a strict domestic violence law making it a felony to commit two or more domestic violence crimes in a twelve-month period. Tex. Penal Code § 25.11. Yet, Texas drastically cut funding for education, mandates an abstinence only sex education curriculum, and requires parental approval before state funded centers can provide teenagers with birth control. Gail Collins, "Mrs. Bush, Abstinence and Texas," *New York Times*, February 16, 2011, www.nytimes.com/2011/02/17/opinion/17gailcollins.html?.
250 Schneider, Battered Women and Feminist Lawmaking, 27–28.

ENDNOTES

251 Editorial, "The Campaign Against Women," *New York Times*, May 20, 2012, http://www.nytimes.com/2012/05/20/opinion/sunday/the-attack-on-women-is-real.html?.
252 White House Council on Women and Girls, "Women in America, Indicators of Social and Economic Well-Being," (2011): 22.
253 Andi Zeisler, Feminism and Pop Culture (Berkely: Seal Press, 2008).
254 White House Council on Women and Girls, "Women in America, Indicators of Social and Economic Well-Being," (2011): 32. Women earn 75% of what men earn.
255 Ibid., 35.
256 Ibid., 13–14. Family households headed by single women outnumber those headed by men with high poverty rates for unmarried female householders.
257 See Hyde Amendment (federal legislation prohibiting federal funding of abortions except in very limited circumstances), affirmed by *Harris v. McRae*, 448 U.S. 297 (1980).; See Rhonda Copelon and Sylvia Law, "Nearly Allied to Her Right "to be"—Medicaid Funding for Abortion: The Story of Harris v. McRae," in Elizabeth Schneider and Stephanie Wildman eds., Women and the Law Stories (New York: Foundation Press, 2011). For a history behind the amendment, discussion of the litigation strategy, and the decision's affect on poor women.
258 *Planned Parenthood v. Casey*, 505 U.S. 833 (1992). Upholding 24 hour waiting requirement in Pennsylvania abortion statute.
259 529 U.S. 598 (2000).
260 545 U.S. 748 (2005). Denying a woman a cause of action against the police for their failure to take action against her abusive husband who ultimately killed their three young daughters.; See Zanita Fenton, "State–Enabled Violence: The Story of the Town of Castle Rock v. Gonzalez," in Schneider and Wildman eds., Women and the Law Stories. For discussion of the Court's reasoning and the consequences for battered women.
261 Inter American Commission on Human Rights, Report No. 80/11 Case 12.626: *Jessica Lenahan (Gonzales) et. al. v. United States*.
262 Susan Faludi, Backlash: The Undeclared War Against American Women (New York: Crown, 1991).